CREDIT SCORE

How to Fix Your Bad Credit Score in 30 Days or Less

(A Practical Guide to Understanding and Improving Your Credit Score)

Joseph Young

Published by Knowledge Icons

Joseph Young

All Rights Reserved

Credit Score: How to Fix Your Bad Credit Score in 30 Days or Less (A Practical Guide to Understanding and Improving Your Credit Score)

ISBN 978-1-990084-74-4

All rights reserved. No part of this guide may be reproduced in any form without permission in writing from the publisher except in the case of brief quotations embodied in critical articles or reviews.

Legal & Disclaimer

The information contained in this book is not designed to replace or take the place of any form of medicine or professional medical advice. The information in this book has been provided for educational and entertainment purposes only.

The information contained in this book has been compiled from sources deemed reliable, and it is accurate to the best of the Author's knowledge; however, the Author cannot guarantee its accuracy and validity and cannot be held liable for any errors or omissions. Changes are periodically made to this book. You must consult your doctor or get professional medical advice before using any of the suggested remedies, techniques, or information in this book.

Upon using the information contained in this book, you agree to hold harmless the Author from and against any damages, costs, and expenses, including any legal fees potentially resulting from the application of any of the information provided by this guide. This disclaimer applies to any damages or injury caused by the use and application, whether directly or indirectly, of any advice or information presented, whether for breach of contract, tort, negligence, personal injury, criminal intent, or under any other cause of action.

You agree to accept all risks of using the information presented inside this book. You need to consult a professional medical practitioner in order to ensure you are both able and healthy enough to participate in this program.

TABLE OF CONTENTS

Introduction

The economic recession of that started in the autumn of 2008 created an unprecedented financial disaster across a wide variety of financial sectors. The impact felt by the ordinary citizen was swift and sudden, and became a nightmare for many ordinary working people who had been "living the American Dream."

While the financial downturn has become global, the credit crunch which resulted from this disaster hit Americans particularly hard because of the great importance that is placed upon having a good credit score in the United States. A person's credit score, and that of their spouse, can now make the difference between getting that great apartment, excellent mortgage or loan rate, or even that wonderful job that you have applied for; or being rejected for all of these fantastic opportunities.

How is this possible? you might ask. Because your credit score is seen as "proof" of how trustworthy and responsible you are. For example, if you wish to work in a bank or other financial institution, but they discover that your credit score is poor or, worse still, that you went through a bankruptcy five years ago, this information will be a red flag for hiring managers. If you can't stay on top of your own finances, the theory runs, how would you ever be able to manage other people's money effectively?

Your credit score can be the difference between you getting that wonderful apartment you want to rent and it going to another couple with a better credit score. It means the difference between a mortgage at a high rate of interest and a low one. Even a fraction of a percentage point on a large loan over several years can cost you thousands if not tens of thousands of dollars more. Your credit score will also affect the size of the down payment you will need to come up with, and the size of the mortgage insurance policy you will be forced to take out if you want the loan.

Many aspiring homeowners in the mid-2000s in the middle of the housing boom thought they were running the numbers correctly, but predatory lending practices, hidden fees, and unexpected administrative and insurance costs such as mortgage insurance soon caused many people to get in over their heads. They thought they would be transforming their rent payments into manageable monthly payments on a valuable asset, only to discover that the repayments were far more than they anticipated, and the value of their home dropped because they had bought at the height of the market and ended up with an "underwater mortgage". In other words, they are paying every month for a house that is worth less than they paid for it and have zero equity in the once seemingly great investment.

They also had to pay more because they were lured with what appeared to be low rates, but were really only for those who had excellent credit scores. People who wanted to refinance their mortgages to get access to the equity they had accumulated in their homes by paying their mortgage regularly also suffered the same fate.

Many of these people are actually lucky in some senses compared with those who lost their homes, not to mention the poor pets who were abandoned or dumped on the streets or into kill shelters all over the country once the recession really started to bite. (And who are still suffering these days as foreclosures continue and the economy in 2014 is still not showing all the signs we had hoped for of a reasonable recovery.)

The rules regarding how to file for bankruptcy have become tighter than ever as debtors, hoping to get off scot free, have been held increasingly accountable for the credit card and other debts that they have run up.

And let's be clear about this. Not everyone who ended up in serious debt was careless. Studies have shown that over 65 percent of bankruptcies being filed in the United States are related to medical bills.

Yes, it is true, some have fallen in to the consumer credit trap in the past 10 years or so. Statistics show that the largest number of credit card offers were mailed within a year of the recession hitting.

Many Americans are suffering financially through no real fault of their own. For many, we are not taught about successful money management in school. We therefore live from pay check to pay check, just managing to scrape through each month. A credit card or two is a tempting way to get what we want NOW, rather than save up for it, but the interest can soon start to add up, making that great bargain at the mall far more expensive than you ever could have imagined.

For some, a sudden financial challenge sends them reeling, and their credit score goes down along with their bank balance and assets. The question then becomes: What is the most rapid way to recover from such a financial disaster?

The good news is that while it does take some time and effort, even the worst credit score can be salvaged provided that you have not declared bankruptcy and are willing to apply focused effort to the process.

As with all of our guides, they are not just for reading, but for taking action. YOU are in charge of your own life and your financial future. Once you understand what your credit score is and the components that go into it, you will be able to take steps to repair it in a systematic and effective way.

Once you improve your credit score, you will start to have access to all of the opportunities you have been missing out on because of past money problems. You may have made mistakes in the past or suffered misfortune, but there is no need for it to haunt you forever.You CAN improve your credit score and your life and take control of your financial future.

In this guide, we will be detailing a number of strategies that have been proven to work that can help you rebuild your credit quickly. In many cases, you should be able to see results within three months and start to feel the benefits of a better credit score in the form of lower interest rates and even less of a credit crunch than you presently might be experiencing.

Let's start now with a look at how credit scores are calculated, so that you can understand your credit score better with a view to improving it using a number of effective strategies.

Chapter 1: Why We Need Credit

Most adults are pretty free to make decisions about how they want to live their lives. They choose where they want to live, the kind of work they want to do and are free to pursue the amount of income they want. But some decisions are made for us. The choice to have credit or not is one of them.

You are told that you have a credit report, not because you wanted it. You didn't contact the credit bureau and ask them to compile a history of your financial activities over the years. People you do not know have quietly submitted personal information about you and collected this data completely without your consent. Then they freely give to anyone who asks, all without your knowledge.

In most cases, the only time you learn about your negative credit report is when you try to make a purchase or something on your own or when you find out that your credit has already been compromised. And once you've struggled with the backlash, experienced all the doors slammed your face, you might even begin to wonder why you should bother at all.

The fact is we live in a society that runs on promises of the future. In fact, our world has created so many obstacles that if you don't have it, it feels like punishment. It separates you from the rest of the community in many ways.

Beyond that, credit is a means of managing your life. Many benefits are to be gained by having credit. People often wonder if it is worth it to have credit. They want to know why we need credit. However, as we've already established, we all have some type of credit whether we want it or not. It is only negative credit that makes life difficult.

Why It Matters

When it comes to making purchases, credit is the primary way that goods are paid for. In this regard, it is an important part of life everyone's life. People use credit cards even when they don't need to, not just because of the convenience and the protection that credit offers.

It is much safer to carry around a credit card than cash when you're out shopping. If your card is stolen, a quick call to the bank and everything is replaced. If your cash is stolen, it's never coming back. But having credit goes further than just a replacement for cash.

It Offers Financial Privileges: More and more often, businesses are withholding special benefits to those who do not have good credit. Your credit gives the rest of the world a picture of your financial health, so they have a good idea of what kind of person you are. With good credit, you can…

Purchase a home: Unless you plan on paying cash for large ticket items like a home or a car, you will need to use credit. While you can make some big-ticket purchases with poor credit, it is going to cost you a lot more. You'll have to pay more interest on the monthly payments. You'll pay more to insure those items, and they will be less forgiving if something happens and you cannot make a payment.

Even if you're not planning to make an immediate purchase, your credit matters. You are often prevented from renting cars, apartments, homes, or equipment when you need them.

Employers now conduct credit checks before they decide if you are trustworthy enough to work in their company. They feel that if you have proven yourself to be financially responsible, you can be responsible enough to handle their assets. They also look at the salary they are offering. If your level of debt is higher than expected for their proposed salary, they may feel you are a risk. Your credit score could prevent you from getting a raise or a promotion as well.

When it comes to getting utilities in your home, you may have difficulty if you don't have a good credit score. You may have to pay a substantial deposit, or you may have to ask someone else to get the lights turned on in your home or apartment.

Unfortunately, almost every aspect of our lives is defined by that same credit score that strangers compile for us, and anyone that wants to do business with us will be focused on our credit and not the kind of person we really are at heart. They don't care that you missed a few payments because you lost your job, or you were in an accident of some kind. They won't care if you now have a new career, or you've just won the lottery. All that matters to them is that mysterious FICO score and what it tells them about you.

Life Without Credit

When you consider that the average American family spends more than $63,000 a year just to meet their basic needs, you can easily understand why credit is so important. However, If you think you can go back to the days of old and live a life 100% credit free you'd be surprised at how difficult it can be. You will find yourself facing even more challenges than you might imagine.

It is a subject that we rarely think about. The world runs on credit, and there is little that can be done about it. Aside from the obvious, mortgages, and auto loans, there are other things that we rely on that are difficult to get without a good credit history.

Nearly every business you deal with will demand credit in some form or another. Even going on vacation without credit is almost impossible. Most hotels now require a credit card even if you plan to pay in cash, and if you want to reserve any activity (tours, recreational events, or even concerts), you will inevitably be asked for a credit card.

Everyone walks around with a cell phone these days. Without a smartphone to connect you to the Internet, you could miss out on a world of opportunities.

Negative credit also makes you feel as if you have never grown up. In our society, a good FICO score is the equivalent as a

13

measure of maturity. It is the evidence that is put before authority figures and rejection feels like a harsh reprimand for not fitting in and following the rules.

Even if you have a good job and are making a decent salary, credit can still hold you back. This impact extends to the psychological level, and you begin to think that it won't matter how good a person you are, how hard you work, or how committed you are to other responsibilities in life that you find you are still not accepted in most circles. The best you can hope for in such circumstances is a circle of friends who do know the kind of person you are and are willing to co-sign for you to get those special privileges. Still, it feels like the ultimate humiliation to go through life struggling to be accepted just because of your credit score.

On a more social level, it causes divisions in your relationships and creates an imbalance of power. This underlying feeling of distrust extends beyond your creditors, but it can affect your personal relationships as well. The struggles you will have with your spouse, your parents, your friends, etc. It can be embarrassing, to say the least, to go to any one of them to ask for money or a loan when you can't get the credit yourself.

Bottom line, while it is possible to go through life without credit, it can be so much better when you have it. This doesn't mean that you need to go out and get into debt. Many people confuse having credit with debt, but these are two different things. Having an established line of credit does not necessarily mean that you must go into debt to keep it. Learning the difference between the two is one of the first things you do when you have a good level of credit management. But even before you can do that, it is important for you to understand that credit report and how it can affect your life.

Chapter 2: How Is A Consumer's

Application Scored?

To illustrate how credit scoring works, consider the following example that uses only three

factors to determine whether someone is creditworthy. (Most systems have 6 to 15 factors.)

Example Monthly income Points Awarded

Less than $400 (0)

$400 to $650 (3)

$651 to $800 (7)

$801 to $1,200(12)

$1,200 + (15)

Age 21-28(11)

28-35(5)

36-48 (2)

48-61 (12)

61 + (15)

Telephone in the home? Yes (12)No (0)

Some credit scoring systems award fewer points to people in their thirties and forties,

because these individuals often have a relatively high amount of debt at that stage of their

lives. The law permits creditors using properly-designed scoring systems to award points

based on age, but people who are 62 or older must receive the maximum number of points

for this factor. If, for example, you needed a score of 25 to get credit, you would need to make

sure you had enough income at a certain age (and, perhaps a telephone) to qualify for credit.

Remember, this example shows very generally how a credit scoring system works. Most

credit scoring systems consider more factors than this example -- sometimes as many as 15 or 20. Usually these factors are obviously related to your credit worthiness. Sometimes,

however, additional factors are included that may seem unusual. For example, some systems

score the age of your car. While this may seem unrelated to creditworthiness, it is legal to use

factors like these as long as they do not illegally discriminate on race, sex, marital status,

national origin, religion, or age.

[OBJ]

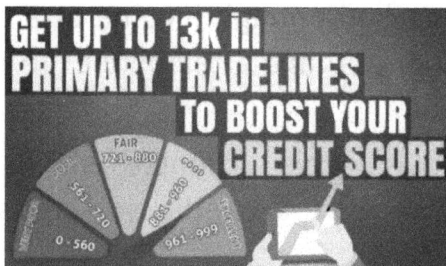

GET UP TO 13k in PRIMARY TRADELINES TO BOOST YOUR CREDIT SCORE

FAIR
721-800
GOOD
831-920
561-720
0-560
961-999

Credit - Foundation For The Future

The importance of good credit cannot be over-emphasized. In today's society credit is no

longer a luxury. It is essential for growth and prosperity. Understand this very important fact

- only 5% of the entire wealth of the world is ever printed as currency. The remaining 95%

exists only on computer chips, in the form of credit. So, if your credit is not good you do not

have access to 95% of the world's wealth. This limits your plans for financial security

drastically. America is rapidly becoming a two-class society in which persons without good

credit (nearly 60% of the population) are treated as second-class citizens. You need not

suffer as a second-class citizen, however. By following the strategies in this manual you can erase bad credit and (re)establish AAA credit, quickly and easily. Understand, however, that

this is only the beginning. Once you have good credit the real work begins. You will have to

act responsibly and with self-discipline to maintain good credit. It can be a formidable battle

unless you know more about what credit is, how to use it properly and how to avoid credit

traps. For this reason we will first discuss these important topics before delving into the

actual methods of restoring or establishing credit.

Credit is the most valuable tool in the world today. Cash doesn't even come in a close second

- but knowledge does. With credit you can obtain just about anything, including investments that will create even greater wealth. Knowledge allows you to make the right choices. For

example, for as little as $20 you can invest in a real estate investment pool. (With R.O.I's of

8% weekly!) With just a few thousand dollars down you can take advantage of the

appreciation and tax advantages of owning a house. You control $100,000 worth of real

estate (and profit from the entire $100,000) while only investing a few thousand.

Without the right knowledge, however, you can never hope to make the financial system

work for you. When 96% of the population fails to achieve financial security it is not due to a

lack of money - again, money is only a tool. Rather, they suffer from a shortage of knowledge that could have helped them to amass wealth. Understand this important concept: Achieving

wealth has nothing to do with collecting dollars, nor is it connected to how much you earn.

All that matters is how you use what you have. There are people who earn over $100,000 a

year and still live from paycheck to paycheck.

There are people who earn less than $12,000 a year who are regularly investing in their

future and will someday have financial security. So do not use the excuse that you just don't

make enough money. Fortunes can be built on very little seed money, and if you really have

what it takes to achieve wealth, you will find a way.

Chapter3: Settling Your Debts"

Settling your debts on your own using creative methods is very possible most people think that you have to hire a credit counselor or credit company you can do this yourself many people do it everyday and are highly successful, first to find out if the debt is still with the original creditors or is it with a collection agency (CA) and to find this out is to simply call the credit card company. If the debt is with the collection agency the original creditor is not going to deal with you the original creditor has received a tax benefit under US law for bad debts, they have cut the ties with the debt, so you would have to deal with the collection agency (CA). Negotiating With Original Creditors 1. Your credit cards have not gone to collections. 2. You are not 150 days late on your payments. 3. Credit card company is still managing

your   accounts.
Negotiating   Tactics
1. How you pay the creditors you may not have a choice to reveal bank information pay with checking account or debit card, however with a collection agency you should never give them your personal financial information some lower level agencies will find ways to pull money out of your account, explain to them that you will pay by check or money order if they send you the invoice.
2. Get the agreement in writing if someone said it verbally then you should assume it did not happen, If it is a collection agency ask them to send a copy for your records having everything in writing saves you from finding out years later that the credit agencies did not honor their   agreement.
3. Negotiating Your credit rating ask for better interest rates if you have established a relationship with the creditor or ask for a higher credit

limit, explain that you have been paying on time and that it would be in their best interest to keep doing business with you use your paying history to your advantage.
4. Confidence when negotiating try to remain confident it is easy to feel pressured or bullied but if you stay on point you will find yourself in good shape do not feel pressure to accept their offer if you can not afford it as long as you get things in writing if it happens to get to court at least you can say you were willing to work with them.
If you can avoid your account going into collections for sure do so, dealing with a collection agency is a headache and then you have to deal with two negatives marks on your credit report, typically after 120 to 150 days credit card companies will send accounts into collections.
Why should a creditor settle with you? Most credit card companies are not willing to talk to consumers until they are

60-90 days down. Disputing Credit Report Information If you receive your credit information and see something incorrect a reason for dispute such as inaccurate information for example, you can remove negative accounts that are still on your credit report after the statue of limitations for debts of seven years passes, Bankruptcies and tax liens maybe included in your report for up to ten years, Filing a dispute must be filed through all three major credit bureaus Equifax, Transunion and Experian each credit report will have a number you will need on your credit dispute letter (example of dispute letter will be later in this book) Equifax you will need a confirmation number, Transunion is a file number, and Experian is a report number, each will ask you provide information such as your address and social security number, and also identify the account that you are disputing and a explanation of why you are disputing the information. Investigation of the disputes the credit bureaus will contact the original creditors listed on the report to find your account, if they cannot find your account or the information is not accurate, they will notify the credit bureau and

the bureau will remove all unverifiable information from your report,The Fair Credit Report Act requires credit bureaus to respond to consumer disputes within 30 days, the credit reporting agencies must investigate all of the disputed

accounts within 5 days after finishing the investigation they must notify the consumer of the results. The bureau can extend the investigation to 45 days if you come up with new information on your behalf during the investigation.

Go to AnnualCreditReport.com

To request your credit report by phone:

Call   1-877-322-8228

You will go through a simple verification process

over   the   phone

Your reports will be mailed to you within

15 days
Allow 2-3 weeks delivery
To request your credit report by mail
Annual Credit Report Request Service
P.O Box 105281
Atlanta, GA 30348-5281
Your reports will be mailed to you within
15 days,
Allow 2-3 weeks delivery
Equifax Credit information Services Inc.
P.O Box 740241
Atlanta GA 30374
Customer care phone: 800-203-7843
Customer.care@equifax.com
Monday-Friday 8am-3am EST
Experian to order my credit report and score
1-888-397-3742
Transunion
to purchase a transunion report:
phone: 800-888-4213
mail: transunion LLC
2 Baldwin Place
P.O Box 1000
Chester, PA 19022
credit disputes 800-916-8800

Monday-Friday   8am-11pm   EST
GOODWILL   LETTER
Date   Your   name
Your   address
City,   State   Zip
Credit   Card   Company
Credit   Card   Company   Address
City,   State   Zip
Re: Acct#xxxx-xxxx-xxxx-xxxx
DEAR   CREDIT   CARD   COMPANY

I've enjoyed being a customer of Bank One since 2000. Today, I'm writing to request a goodwill adjustment to my credit files. I was good customer from the time I received my credit card in 2000 until 2011 when I suffered a medical illness which wrecked my finances and my ability to make timely credit card payments. As a result I fell behind on my payments by 60 days. Fortunately, I was able to turn things around and I've been timely with my payments ever since.

I'm preparing to shop for a house and was told those late payments will keep me from getting the best interest rate. I'm requesting a goodwill adjustment since the payments do not reflect my current payment status, Thank you for your time reading this letter and the consideration you've given my situation.

Sincerely
Your   Name
Remember to keep it short and to the point, (that was just an example of a Goodwill   Letter)
Dispute   letter
Date
Your   Name
Your   Address
Your   City,   State,   Zip   code
Complaint   Department
Name   of   Credit   Bureau
Address
City, State, Zip code Dear Sir or Madam

I am writing to dispute the following information on my file. (just make copies of all your records that you send) the disputed items are circled the items are identified as (name of credit card company and ac#) and I am disputing it is inaccurate and incomplete. I am requesting the item be deleted and corrected (describe what you have sent copies or documents supporting my stance, please investigate this matter and delete or correct the disputed item as soon as possible.

Sincerely

Your name

RECAP

1. Explained " what is a credit score"?

2. Where can you get your credit reports for free.

3. Good and Bad credit scores. 4. The two quickest ways to raise your credit scores.

5. How to start the rebuilding process of your credit.

6. Methods on settling your debts.

7. When to negotiate with creditors and negotiating tactics.

8. How to get your credit report information.

9. How to dispute your credit report information.

10. Contact Information of all the Credit Bureaus.

11. How to write a Goodwill letter to your Creditors. 12. How to write a Dispute letter to the Bureaus

Chapter 4: Disputing Any Credit Report

Errors In 30 Days

The Correct Ways to Dispute an Error Reported To the Credit Bureau by a Business/Financial Institution

The previous chapter touched on errors, and the act of disputing them to make things right.

It is quite common for credit reports to contain errors. There are so many things that could show up on your credit report that have no business being there- from accounts that are not yours to inaccurate late payments to falsely reported bankruptcy even.

The previous chapter shows you how to examine your credit report for errors that may be dragging your score down. This chapter will show you how to dispute errors with credit bureaus, as well as several things you need to know.

Here is an overview on some errors that you can dispute:

Payments that are reported as late, which you actually paid on time

Accounts that are not yours

Creditors that are inaccurate

Credit account balances that are inaccurate

Loan limit amounts that are inaccurate

Account status that are reported inaccurately. For instance, an account status, which is reported as past due when actually, the account is current

How Do You Go About Making Your Dispute?

Step 1: Ensure That Your Disputes Are Legitimate

If your gripe is with negative items that you are at fault for and as such, are only errors in so far as YOU made them, Chapter 4 will show you how to fix mistakes you are at fault for. It will be a mistake to try to dispute these- once the credit bureau puts a black mark on you for frivolous disputes, this is the opinion they will hold of you and you will go through extra scrutiny. Sometimes, you will even have previously deleted items re-included, as is mentioned in Step 3.

Here are some other tips:

Do not just file a dispute for every single thing on your report at a go. Many people think that the way to make large scale changes and boost their credit score quickly is to dispute everything. What you don't know is that the credit bureau has every right to deem your dispute as lacking in logic and will surely reject your entire dispute even without a second look at it.

Do not file all disputes at a go.

In fact, if you want to dispute an item more than once, make sure to have a different reason for every dispute so that the credit bureau does not think that you are merely blowing hot air by sending in duplicates. It has the right to deem you as frivolous, should this happen and will be acting perfectly within its rights if it rejects your dispute altogether.

Step 2: Decide Which One Of The 3 Available Ways You Will Use To Make Your Dispute

You have 3 options to make your dispute through:

Dispute online

Dispute via mail

Dispute over the phone

To dispute online or over the phone, it will be necessary for you to have ordered a credit report copy within the last 30 days. You will also be required to give your credit report number.

How To Dispute Your Credit Report Errors Online

Disputing your errors online is quite convenient, and it takes very little time as well. However, there are a few drawbacks, one of them being that you can only get the results of the dispute online. You will not get results by mail, which robs you of the paper trail that you may need in the future if the credit bureau fails to act or respond in a manner that is appropriate to your rights. It gets even more unappealing- you will have to mail in necessary documentation or proof to support your dispute, even as you dispute online.

However, you know what applies best to you and if you believe disputing online is the way to go, here is how to dispute with all 3 credit report companies and the links to follow:

How to dispute online on Equifax

If you believe that any item in the credit report that you get from Equifax is either incomplete or inaccurate, visit https://www.**equifax**.com/personal/**disputes** and click on the "Submit a dispute" button. The first step will be to log in. After this, follow the guidelines provided on the page, taking care to follow the directives provided in this chapter. Hit the "Submit" button when you are through.

If you need to check your dispute status, simply visit the same link and click on the "Check Status" button.

How to dispute online on TransUnion

To dispute your credit report on TransUnion, visit https://dispute.transunion.com and just like is the case on Equifax, click the provided "Submit a dispute" button provided. After that, log in; follow the submission steps provided on the page, all of which are very straightforward, and fill in all the necessary details, taking care to follow the directives provided in this. After you are through, hit the "Submit" button.

How to dispute online on Experian

The process here is very much like that of Equifax and TransUnion. You will visit this link: https://www.experian.com/disputes/main.html. Right at the top of the page, you will find "Start a new dispute online" and "Check the status of an existing dispute" buttons as well as a "View results of a completed dispute". To start a new dispute, click the "Start a new dispute online" button, log in and follow the very straightforward step by step guidelines provided on the page before submitting.

Disputing Your Credit Report Errors Via Mail

This will take more time than it does when you dispute online. However, it provides you with the necessary paper trail that you would need if the credit bureau fails to heed to your rights by either responding late or failing to respond altogether.

Credit bureaus have 30 days to carry out an investigation and respond to your dispute. The most they can wait before responding is 45 days, and this is only allowed if you send in additional proof supporting your claim. If they refuse to respond in that time, then by all means sue them. You have the right to sue in Federal Court for up to $1,000.

Here are a few details that you need to know about dispute letters:

When you write to the bureaus, always make sure that you include your identification information, such as your name, address and SSN.

Make sure your letter is short and concise. You should not write more than a few sentences, as you will see on the sample letters.

It is enough to simply state the reason why you believe a certain item is erroneous (i.e. I was not late as I paid on this date) and request that corrections be made

The credit bureaus have 30 days to process your dispute and reply accordingly. To make things easy, it is important to be brief and direct.

Mail is often very effective- often more than online disputes. Why is this? Well, snail mail will take several days to arrive to the bureau, and several more days to get processed and delivered to the relevant office. However, your mailing date is as relevant as ever, and the 30 day countdown begins on the very day you send your letter. The short time window will prompt the bureau to attend to your dispute immediately. When you dispute online, they get your dispute immediately, and they can afford to set it aside while they take care of other things. There are also too many people disputing online.

It will help to be persistent. If the first try fails to work, try again and again. However, ensure that these letters are not duplicates of each other or else they will dismiss your disputes on frivolous grounds

The dispute addresses to the 3 credit bureaus are provided at the Chapter's end. These addresses will deal specifically with dispute mails.

When you dispute via mail:

Write a letter explaining the information that you feel should be removed

Include the reasons as to why that detail is accurate

Include a copy of proof of the particular error

Send your letter via certified mail with a return receipt requested so that you have proof of exactly when you made the dispute and when your creditor receives it

Keep track of the time that has passed

Disputing Credit Report Errors By Phone

You will follow the same format as you did when disputing via mail, except this time, you will detail your dispute and reasons why it should stand over a phone conversation. However, it will be even better if you follow up your phone conversation by mailing in a copy of proof of the error in place.

Types of proof that you can send with your credit report

You can only get the stuff you want removed from your credit report removed if you provide proof. Ideally, some of the types of proof that you can send include:

A recent utility bill or bank statement

A copy of your social security card

A copy of driver's license

A cancelled check showing that you actually paid a given bill on time

A recent billing statement showing your balance and credit card limit

Only send in copies of your documents. Keep the originals with you.

Step 3: Wait For The Credit Bureau Response To Your Credit Report Dispute

The credit reporting agency may then reply to your dispute by simply deleting whatever information you had disputed with immediate effect. However, they reserve the right to re-insert previously deleted items, if those very items are later verified. They have to notify you that they have put the items back though, and they have to do it in writing.

Here is a sample phrasing for a dispute letter:

Sample 1:

I have reviewed my credit report copy and I have found an error with GE Capital Account XXX-XXX-XXXX-1254. This account has been listed as being 30 days late. On the contrary, I have not been late on this account at any one time. Kindly do away with this inaccurate information.

Sample 2

I have reviewed my credit report copy and I have found several negative accounts, which are older than 7 years. These are the accounts that you should remove:

- NHSKKA/Express XXX-XXX-XXX
- Verizon Visa XX-XXXX-XXXX-XXX

Dispute Addresses for the Major Credit Bureaus

Experian
Dispute Department
P.O. Box 9701
Allen, TX 75013

Trans Union
Consumer Solutions
P.O. Box 2000
Chester, PA 19022-2000

Equifax
P.O. Box 7404256
Atlanta, GA 30374-0256

Next, we will discuss how to improve your credit score even with the items that are accurately reported on your credit report.

Chapter 5: Negotiating/Settlement Chart:

Timing Is Everything!!!

In this chapter, we will be going through the stages of the settlement. By the end, you will be able to understand "every debt **is not** created equal."

The negotiation and settlement process is contingent on several factors:

*Type of debt

*Amount owed

*Age of the delinquency account

*The Creditor/Collection Company

*The Stage of delinquency referenced in the timeline below

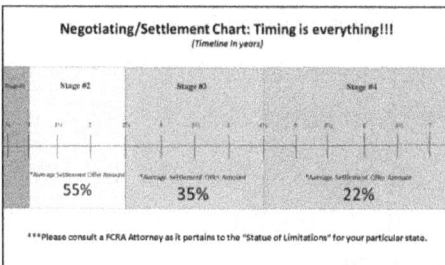

Negotiating/Settlement Chart: Timing is everything!!!
(Timeline in years)

Stage #1	Stage #2	Stage #3	Stage #4
	Average Settlement Offer Amount 55%	*Average Settlement Offer Amount* 35%	*Average Settlement Offer Amount* 22%

***Please consult a FCRA Attorney as it pertains to the "Statue of Limitations" for your particular state.

(0 to 1 Years) Stage One - The beginning of the timeline represents the "original date of delinquency." At the beginning of this phase is typically when the Original Creditor has your debt and has not sold it to a 3rd party Collection Company or attorney. It's recommended, as soon as you become aware of an immediate or forth coming crisis, call your creditors. Explain the situation to them in order to see what options may be eligible for you.

For example, if a factory plant is considering closing down in a few months, pick up the phone immediately and inform all your creditors. In turn, they will notate your file and go over all your possible options.

Please Note: I will never advocate anyone just to throw their hands up in regards to debt. This strategy, in the long run, will more than likely back fire and cause more damage than good.

When trying to negotiate in Stage One, bear in mind that their ultimate strategy is to collect and recover as much money back as possible. Creditors will customarily reverse late fees or reduce other penalties and interest with the purpose of collecting as much as possible as soon as possible. If there were ever a moment of time to set up a payment plan, it would fall within this phase with the original creditor.

Please Note: If you have the funds available to start a payment plan or strike a settlement then follow the settlement strategies of Stage Two. It is better to handle debts quicker rather than later if possible, since so many things are hanging on your credit such as employment, insurance, etc...

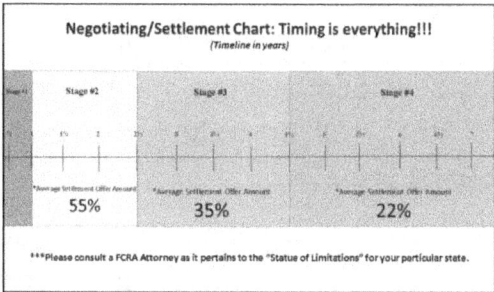

Negotiating/Settlement Chart: Timing is everything!!!
(Timeline in years)

(1 to 2½ Years) Stage Two – Midway through Stage One and entering into Stage Two is when a Collection Company or attorney can get your account depending on the type of debt. The reason it is recommended to pursue a payment plan or quick settlement within the first phase of (0 to 1 Years) is because historically, most payment plan don't work after Stage One. In this period, the average amount is around 55% of the total debt. A strategy to help you achieve this percentage or an even lower settlement amount is to first have at least 60% of the total debt in assessable cash. This strategy will give you the confidence to know that if an offer is presented low enough you can take advantage of it. You never want to call to negotiate a settlement without having the money available because some offers only go for that call or only for a few days afterward.

In order to stay organized, best practices prove that taking detailed notes on the actual collection statement will keep everything together and simplified. When you call them, let them know that you are calling the Collection Companies on your credit report attempting to settle while you have the opportunity "today" to do so.

Let your first offer be as low as 30% of the total amount. Then be silent, giving them the opportunity to talk next. Your silence speaks louder than any word or words you can think. Remember, whoever talks the most loses. With them paying pennies on end, your true confidence should come from that you have the cash available, and they need to close out this account as quick as possible. Presenting a win-win situation for everyone makes for an effective strategy.

As long as the counter-offer stays around 55% and doesn't go over, then you want to follow the counseled steps below in its entirety:

Steps #1 - Verbally ask for written confirmation on their letterhead, stating the settlement terms which needs to include the following language:

Step #2 - Their agency confirms the agreement that the payment of ($_____) is to pay the settled debt in full which is connected to the following account #: _____.

Step #3 - Their agency confirms that they will report that this account is "Paid as Agreed" on all three Credit Bureaus and after receiving this payment their agency will not:

*Re-age the debt, nor

*Create a new account number

Please Note: Collection Companies try to use tactics such as re-aging debts or creating new account numbers to manipulate the process for their benefit.

On the other hand, if they do not make a reasonable counter-offer around 55% of the debt, then request that they notate your file that they are rejecting your money and hang up. Record the time, date, and the representative's information on the collection statement and then go to the next Collection Company. Place this collection debt at the bottom of the collection pile, that gives them another opportunity only after all the other collection Companies have been given a chance first.

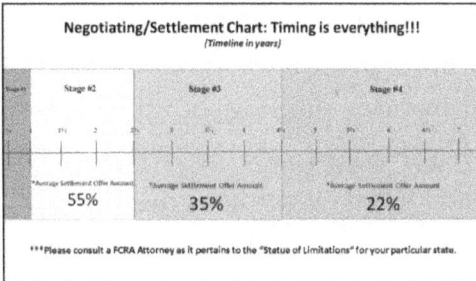

Negotiating/Settlement Chart: Timing is everything!!!
(Timeline in years)

Stage #1	Stage #2	Stage #3	Stage #4
Average Settlement Offer Amount **55%**		*Average Settlement Offer Amount* **35%**	*Average Settlement Offer Amount* **22%**

***Please consult a FCRA Attorney as it pertains to the "Statue of Limitations" for your particular state.

(2½ to 4½ Years) Stage Three – Between the range of 2½ to 4½ Years is when a Collection Company is thinking about the Statue of Limitations and realize that time is running against them. The link below which was produced by Bankrate.com shows the Statue of Limitations for each state.

[Click here for the Statue of Limitations for each State]

51

***Please consult a FCRA Attorney as it pertains to the "Statue of Limitations" for your particular state for more information.

After reviewing the link and seeing your state's Statute of Limitations, you will discover that most open-ended accounts (i.e. credit card, etc.) start having a Statute of Limitations limit around three years. There are some states with exceptions, such as West Virginia and Rhode Island that have limits of 10 years. With this in mind, it will give you more confidence in settling and negotiating with Collection Companies for an amount around 35% of the total debt for Stage Three. Similarly to the strategy in Stage Two, you would want to start off with a settlement offer around 25% of the total debt and then be silent.

As a reminder for Stage Three, as long as the counter-offer stays around 35% and doesn't go over, then you want to follow the counseled steps below in its entirety:

Steps #1 - Verbally ask for written confirmation on their letterhead, stating the settlement terms which needs to include the following language:

Step #2 - Their agency confirms the agreement that the payment of ($_____) is to pay the settled debt in full which is connected to the following account #:

Step #3 - Their agency confirms that they will report that this account is "Paid as Agreed" on all three Credit Bureaus and after receiving this payment their agency will not:

*Re-age the debt, nor

*Create a new account number

Conversely, if they do not make a reasonable counter-offer around 35% of the debt, then request that they notate your file that they are rejecting your money and as a result ending the call. Record the time, date, and the representative's information on the collection statement and then go to the next Collection Company. Place this collection debt at the bottom of the collection pile which gives them another opportunity only after all the other

Collection Companies have been given a chance first.

Commit to memory, Collections Companies pay pennies on end for the debt and their profits are produced by the more you pay.

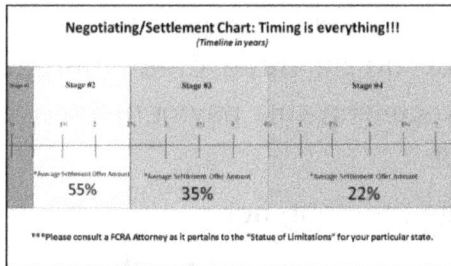

Negotiating/Settlement Chart: Timing is everything!!!
(Timeline in years)

Stage #1	Stage #2	Stage #3	Stage #4
	Average Settlement Offer Amount 55%	*Average Settlement Offer Amount* 35%	*Average Settlement Offer Amount* 22%

**Please consult a FCRA Attorney as it pertains to the "Statue of Limitations" for your particular state.

(4½ to 7 Years) Stage Four – This is the last phase but a unique stage because as you will see with the Statue of Limitations chart, individual states such as Kentucky has limits that can last up to 15 years!!! With this in mind, Stage Four is only an average timeframe for majority of the states.

In general, Collection Companies are aware of the fact that they have the right to sue you for the debt, but only until your state's State of Limitations concludes. This truth is why the settlement amount for Stage Four is 22% which means that your initial offer should be around 11% of the debt.

Considering all factors, if you have a outstanding debt of five years with an amount of $1,000 then you should reject any settlement offer over $220. You should prepare to hang up the phone and tell them you will go to the next Collection Company on your credit report with hopes of settling. Then call the next collection Company to see their mindset.

What about Judgments?

As it pertains to settling or negotiating a judgment, best practices from interviewing legal professionals' state, first go to a courthouse and obtain your "Credit File" in regards to the judgment. After reviewing your file, contact the closest FCRA Attorney in your state to ask them these three most important questions:

Question #1 - What is the maximum number of years a judgment can be "Enforced" within your state?"

Question #2 - Does your state allow Judgments to become "Renewable?"

Question #3 - What is the "Maximum Interest Rate" allowed on a Judgment for your state?

The FCRA Attorney's fee structure is "Fee Contingency Based" which means a payment is only made if the lawyer wins your case in court.In fact, the legal professionals I have interviewed actually encouraged me to inform clients to talk to an FCRA Attorney to get both the right legal guidance and their specific questions answered as it pertains to their judgments.

In essence, a judgment signifies that legal proceedings have already started against you- so why wouldn't you want to get your own legal advice!!!

(Click here to be directed to the steps to find a FCRA Attorney)

Points to remember:

* I will never advocate just throwing your hands up and walk away from debt. This strategy, in the long run, will more than likely backfire and cause more damage than good.

*Remember- "You Are The Best Person for The Job"

*Collection Companies pay pennies on end in order to make a profit because they understand that, "every debt **is not** created equal."

In the next chapter, I will cover a car owner's worst nightmare. You will discover a secret that could ruin your credit as well as **"all"** your checking and savings accounts...

Chapter 6: Understanding The Jargon:

Complicated Financial Words Explained

One of the reasons that many people avoid credit cards all together is because of the countless confusing terms that exist within the realm of money borrowing.This being the case, if you're apprehensive about moving forward with establishing your credit score because of the chance that you'll end up confused and in a position where you're making decisions based on little knowledge of terms and conditions that exist within credit card terms and conditions, you're not alone. This chapter will focus on defining the frequently used terms that are used by banks who offer credit cards as an option for payment. It would be a shame for you to never get a credit card because you are unsure of how their conditions will influence your life. Plus, when used correctly, credit cards can help to alleviate instead of burden your wallet by freeing up some space for more money flow. Let's take a look at some of these terms that seek understanding.

Term 1: Annual Fee

If you're just starting out establishing credit for yourself and are beginning to research the different types of credit cards that exist, you should be weary of the words "annual fee". This means that the bank who owns the credit card will charge you a yearly fee in order to use their services. This fee can range from as little as fifteen dollars to as much as three hundred dollars. When you're first starting out, there's really no real reason why you should be paying a fee in order to use a credit card. Later in life, when you've established your credit and have been accepted to use a credit card that offers great rewards in exchange for charging a yearly rate, it would be a good idea at this time to consider paying a bank a yearly fee to use their services.

Term 2: Annual Percentage Rate

Every credit card lender is required to disclose what their annual percentage rate (more commonly seen as APR) will be for a given card. This percentage is a reflection of the percentage of interest that a bank will charge their customer when there is a balance left in their credit card account at the end of each month. As we saw in the previous chapter, if you pay off your credit card purchases each month in full, you will never be exposed to your card lender's APR rate because there will be no balance for them to charge interest against. It's important to look at what a card's APR is before applying to use it.

Term 3: Balance Transfer

A balance transfer is a term that's often used as a promotional vehicle for a credit card lending company. Specifically, this is when debt from one credit card is transferred to another credit card. A promotion of this type might consist of one bank promising that if you transfer your debt from one bank to theirs, you won't pay interest on this money for a certain amount of time. Before engaging in this type of deal, you have to make sure that you know exactly when interest will start to accrue on this money at the new bank. Often, once the interest-free period expires, the interest rate for this money skyrockets. The customer is left paying far more than when their money was in their previous bank. If you keep a good handle on your money and often pay back your purchases in full at the end of each month, it's possible to avoid the concept of balance transfers all together.

Term 4: Minimum Payment

A minimum payment refers to the minimum amount that a cardholder must pay against their balance at the end of each month. If this minimum amount is not met by the end of the month, you will be charged interest against your credit card payment and you risk defaulting on your credit card. This means that you will no longer be able to use it. The minimum payment is typically calculated at two percent of the current outstanding balance. Keep this in mind when you're making payments, as this minimum can add up quickly.

Term 5: Cash Advance Fees

When discussing the subject of cash advance fees, the best advice up front is to say that cash advances should generally be avoided by a consumer. A cash advance works similarly to the withdrawal of money through a debit card account in the sense that you will receive paper money immediately after withdrawing the funds; however, a cash advance differs from a debit card in the senses that a cash advance from a credit card company means that this paper money immediately accrues interest as soon as it reaches your hands. The average percentage rate that it costs to take out a cash advance is usually either two percent of the cash advance, or ten dollars if ten dollars is greater than the two percent rate. This means that if you take out one hundred dollars as a cash advance, the bank will automatically take ten dollars from your advance because two percent of one hundred dollars is only two dollars. In this example, the bank is taking ten percent of your cash advance. Relatively speaking, that is a significant chunk of interest. Additionally, when this type of transaction occurs, the bank usually takes the interest money directly from the cash advance. This means that you will end up only receiving ninety dollars at the time of your advance. These conditions make a cash advance particularly expense.

Term 6: Credit Limit

A credit limit refers to the amount of money that a credit card company will lend you. You can easily see how much the lending company is willing to give to your card in its entirety on your credit card statement or on the online portals that are now easily accessible to the general public. Often, the limit on your credit is subtracted to include any outstanding balances that you have on your credit card during a given period. The most important factor that will determine your credit limit is how much money you make in a year. This makes sense. A credit card company is not going to give you nearly enough money to exceed how much you make in a year. This being the case, it's important to not open many credit cards at once and then be unable to pay them back because you have too many other credit card accounts. Pay attention and respect your credit limits. An even better idea is to never come close to maxing out your credit card to its full limit.

Chapter 7: What Not To Do When You Fix

Your Credit

Now that we looked at the things you can do to repair your credit, in this chapter, we look at the things that you must not do as it will further worsen your credit score.

Working without a plan

If you start out without a plan, then you are sure to go wrong. Never do anything without a plan as it will make it very difficult for you. Before you decide to start repairing your credit, sit down and draw a plan of action for yourself and try to stick to it till you are done. You can start by writing down your debts and the money you have and then move to looking at how much you must save to pay it off fully etc. That way, you will not end up wasting any money and be able to pay off your debts faster.

Not paying bills on time

One of the worst things you could do is to not pay your bills on time. You might think that you will be able to save some money by paying late but that will be a wrong idea. Remember that 35% of your total credit score will be made up by your payment history and anything that you pay late or not pay will bring down your credit considerably. If you like, you can install an app that reminds you to pay a bill every month. Try and pay it off on the first day itself so that you don't forget about it later.

Borrowing hefty loan

When you are already under stress for bad credit, don't try to worsen it by borrowing a hefty loan. This loan might be for personal reasons or to pay off the debts. But if you were unable to pay off your debts on previous borrowings, then you won't be able to pay it off on this borrowing. So don't be tempted to borrow from banks or lenders, who might charge you exorbitant interest rates and cause further damage to your credit score.

Approaching a firm to help

If you think that a company will be really interested in helping you out without charging you a hefty amount for their service, then you are absolutely wrong. Any company will try to squeeze out more and more money from you, which will put you in a bad position. And if it is doing something for free, then it might not be sound advice that is being given. Don't rush to avail the help of a firm as the very first thing. Wait for some time and do everything that you can to repair your credit. If still it is not happening, then you can approach them.

Using cards to splurge

The last thing you want is to use your credit card to try and buy all the good and expensive things. Many people will think that it is not nice for them to not splurge on something as it can affect their social status. But that thought will have a devastating impact on your credit score. You will have a score that might cause you to lose your cards altogether and not have the opportunity to apply for a new one. You must therefore control all your urges to splurge and try to curb your expenses wherever possible.

Distress sale

When you have a bad score, you must not go crazy and start selling everything that is valuable to you, just to raise enough money. You might end up undergoing loses while doing so. You can instead hold on to the item and borrow money from a friend or family. Once the price of the item goes up, you can sell it for money and repay the sum you borrowed and keep the rest as your profit.

Filing bankruptcy

Filing for bankruptcy should never be an option for you. You must control all urge to do so and even if you are advised to do so, you must consider other options. You can undergo financial counselling and understand how you can lessen your debt and pull you out of the bad credit state. If you file for bankruptcy once, then you will find it extremely difficult to build a good credit again and not have the means to erase out that one bankruptcy stain from your credit score.

Cancelling old cards

Never cancel your oldest cards. If you have to, then you must cancel your latest credit cards. If you cancel old ones, then you will end up clearing a lot of your payment history from your report and end up shortening it. That will not be good as you might have made timely payments before and your history on that card might have been good.

Keeping track

Not keeping track of your moves can be a wrong thing to do. So always keep track of your every move. Maintain a journal and write down your expenses, your payments, your borrowings etc. That way, you will know exactly where you stand at any given point in time and you will have a handy reference for you to check immediately when asked by a bank or creditor.

Chapter 8: Make A Plan

Author's note: In this chapter we will explore the critical importance of building and maintaining a budget. For step by step instructions the "Credit Friendly Budget Guide" is available at: www.FinancialEmpowermentServices.com /credit-friendly/

If you plan for nothing you're certain to accomplish it.

Do you have hopes for your future? Would you like to earn more money? Would you like to travel? Would you like to spend more time with your family and friends

Everyone says "yes" to these types of questions. We all have wishes, dreams and aspirations. And if you follow up these questions with another one - "Have you ever set goals to make these happen?" - many people will say that they have. However, if you ask "Have you budgeted for any of it?" - the answer is typically "no".

"Budget" is a word of universal dread. Over half of Americans neither plan for nor manage their monthly expenses, and though the reasons why are not clearly understood, here are some top reasons I've uncovered from conversation with clients over the years:

"I use every penny every month and don't have enough money to budget."

"I make more than enough money to cover my expenses and don't need to budget."

"A budget is a cage that strips away my freedom to choose how and when I spend my money."

"The budget I keep in my head is good enough."

"It's too much hassle."

These may all sound reasonable. Some of them even contain grains of truth. However, the greater truth is that, for most of us, these are justifications we use to avoid having to face the harsh reality of our financial habits. Let's consider each of them in turn:

The myth: "I don't have enough money to budget."

When you are scraping by every month and you don't spend on extravagance it is easy to question the value of a budget. That's why this justification works so well. Why bother to plan what you spend when every penny is already accounted for? But the reality is that **identifying priorities and establishing the discipline to stick to a budget are precisely the skills which allow someone to grow beyond a paycheck to paycheck life and into financial abundance.**

The myth: "I make enough money, I don't need to budget."

This is another easily believed argument, that masks two very different concerns:

One is the suspicion that perhaps I **don't** actually make enough money. Many of us have lived beyond our means by making up the difference with credit cards, advances on payroll or by simply ignoring our bills. While the acknowledgment of this can be difficult, the benefit of knowing the truth of our position is powerful.

The second concern is: fear of failure. As international best selling author Jim Collins wrote: "Good is the enemy of Great." For those whose lives are comfortable, or even just passable, why risk it? The reason why can only be determined by you. What would make your life great? How determined are you to make that happen?

The myth: "A budget strips me of my freedom."

This is one of my favorite excuses, because it's at least partially true. There is an element of freedom that's lost when you constrain your purchases through a budget. But it's not quite that simple.

The budgeting process itself is a 'free' choice. We choose to budget, not to punish ourselves, but to lay a path toward even greater financial independence and the greater 'freedoms' that come with it.

In addition, most purchases that we would defend with the 'freedom' argument are not as free as we think. We typically use this argument to defend our impulse purchases, purchases that are otherwise difficult to justify.

Budgeting does not eliminate freedom, it frees us from mental slavery. Through budgeting you can build your own freely chosen path to financial independence!

The myth: "I keep it in my head."

As a college student this seemed a perfectly logical argument. Like most college students, I had an ATM budget. If the ATM gave me money, "yay." If not, "darn." If you're living to the last penny every month some variation of the ATM budget might seem to work for you as well. But it's really just a way to cover up any and all of the preceding fears.

In addition, one's head is also the source of all our impulse purchases. It is far too easy to justify unnecessary purchases through quick mental games. The head is a dangerous place to keep one's budget.

A budget is not just knowing how much is in the bank. A budget is a goal setting process. It is through budgeting that you establish priorities for your life and build a plan to make them happen. If you care about your future write it down.

The myth: "It's too much hassle."

This is certainly the most honest of the justifications. It is more of a hassle to create a budget than to ignore it. However, the substantial, life changing impact of a budget is more than worth the hassle to create it.

So how do you budget?

It's a simple process. In its most basic form we determine our after tax income and subtract from it our monthly expenditures. The challenge comes in prioritizing expenses. The categories we use for this purpose were introduced in the last chapter:

- Mandatory Expenses
- Savings
- Carefully Considered Desires
- Non-crucial Desires

-        Unnecessary   Expenses
-          Unnecessary   Fees
- Personal Investment

If you conduct a thorough expense review from chapter 3 you will have determined your existing expenses. You can also start today by recording, for one month, every purchase and logging that expense in one spot. The process of recording your expenditures increases your awareness of them.

Once you have these identified, it is then time to begin making choices. Your expenses have to fit your income. If they don't you'll either need to increase your income or reduce your expenses. To make this happen you may find, after some serious consideration, that your non-crucial desires are unnecessary and your carefully considered desires aren't as crucial as you once thought.

Some healthy habits to consider:

- Pay yourself first. After your mandatory expenses are determined transfer some percentage of your income to savings —

10% if you can. If that is too much, make it a smaller amount. But establish the practice of saving something every month.

- Eliminate one unnecessary habit each month. Whether it's drinking too much pop or eating out too often, focus on changing one dis-empowering activity every month.

- Make a habit of thrift. Reducing spending does not have to feel restrictive. Though it goes against our cultural bias for 'new' and 'shiny', the search for deals can be enjoyed, even celebrated once you change your attitude toward it.

There are numerous tools to help you budget. If you are comfortable on the computer you can use prepackaged budget templates or create your own using these common spreadsheet programs:

- Microsoft Excel
- Open Office Spreadsheet
- Google Doc Spreadsheet

If you prefer to use pencil and paper, check your local office supply store for budgeting worksheets. You can also download the Credit Friendly Budget Guide mentioned at the start of this chapter.

Stick to it!

It's hard work. But it is perhaps the most important work anyone can undertake for their financial future. Budgeting is not just the ins and outs of monthly spending. Budgeting is a key element in setting life goals. It should not be drudgery, but instead an opportunity to explore your dreams and map the paths to achieve them.

Recommendations to help you **Make a Plan:**

1. Ignore the myths which would keep you from budgeting. The benefits of doing so far outweigh any justifications not to.

2. Be strong when assessing your carefully considered and non-crucial desires. Much money which is currently allotted to these categories could be more meaningfully applied elsewhere.

3. Budgeting is the first step toward true financial maturity. Make a budget. Stick to it. Live an intentional life.

Chapter 9: I Have Bad Credit. Now, What?

If you have bad credit there are several steps you can take to make sure you turn it around as quickly as possible.

Step One – Make sure your information is accurate.

The first step to cleaning credit is to make sure that your credit profile is accurate. We start off by requesting a free credit report, from each bureau, by going to www.annualcreditreport.com. These reports are free, by federal law, and will not be counted as an inquiry on your profile. Since you will get a separate report from each of the three bureaus, you will know who is reporting what and to whom. Very important. Now review each report for accuracy and duplication. Is your name spelled correctly? Are all of your addresses correct? Are there any duplications? Many times your lender will sell your loan to a collection company and now the debt will show up twice or more times. We will talk about how to correct your information later in this chapter.

Step Two – Pay off negative accounts

The collection, past due, charge-offs, tax liens and so forth are negative accounts and need to be paid off if you want to re-establish your good credit. But not all accounts should be paid.

Take a look at when the lender has last reported the account to the bureau. The normal collection, past due, and charge-off accounts will only remain on your credit profile for 7 years. Bankruptcies, tax liens, and other public records will remain for 10 years. If your lender has reported your account as a charge-off but has not updated the information in the past few years then there is a chance that they will not ever update it and ignoring the account may be the best thing to do. Let sleeping dogs lie. Remember that time is your friend and that the older the negative comments are, the less value they have on your score.

If your lender is reporting the negative information regularly or currently then you will need to deal with it. The best option is to talk to the lender and see if they would be willing to remove the account from your credit report in exchange for payment. This is optional to them, they are not required to do so. But it cannot hurt to ask, especially if it is a collection company. You may also want to ask for a discount in exchange for a full payment. It is rare when a collection company will be willing to give you both the discount and the removal from your credit, but those that do not ask will never receive, so ask away. Also, make sure that whatever agreement you negotiate is given to you, in writing, prior to you making any payment. Once you have the agreement in writing, make sure you follow thru with your part of the bargain. If you know that you will not have the money until 15 days from now then negotiate that your payment will be made 30 days after the agreement is reached. Everything is negotiable at this point.

If your lender sold the account to a collection company, and both are reporting the account, make sure that the original lender shows that the account was transferred and has the correct date of the transfer. This will get rid of the duplication of bad credit.

If the negative information is already paid off or is a public record, such as a bankruptcy or tax lien which is paid off, make sure that the final status of the account is correct in status and date on your profile. If you have a bankruptcy, does it state that it was discharged? Is the discharge date correct? Do the accounts that were discharged by the bankruptcy show the filing date of the bankruptcy as their final date? Do these accounts show a zero balance? If you had a tax lien, does it show that it was released (paid off)? Is the date of release correct? If the paid off account is a collection or charge-off, is the paid off date correct?

Once you have cleared up your bad credit as much as possible then you should go back to chapter 3 on how to start your credit profile, the steps are the same in order to re-establish your credit. But do the clean-up first. You would not cook a dessert, in the same pot that you cooked a stew, without cleaning it out thoroughly first. It's the same thing here.

To clear up information on your credit profile, send a DISPUTE letter to the bureaus needing corrections. Most of the bureaus have a dispute entry page on their website but if you can't find it or would rather do it in writing, their addresses are in Chapter 10.

I would highly suggest that all disputes be done online directly with the bureaus. Written requests will need you to include your social security number and date of birth. If these letters were to get lost in the mail, who knows what may happen to this information. Dispute requests may also be done thru your account with www.annualcreditreport.com.

Can't find the right credit cards or other info, go to

www.fix-my-score.com

Chapter 10: How To Settle Debts.

While creditors would like you to think otherwise, the fact of the matter is that any debt that you have is negotiable. What's more, regardless of the amount, 90 percent of creditors are going to be willing to take a lump sum now over a promise to pay at a later date. When it comes to negotiating large amounts, the following tips may make it easier to come out ahead.

Have a story and stick with it: The person you are dealing with isn't going to be interested in your life story, but they will need to know why you are unable to pay in full right now. This means you are going to want to have a story that outlines your hardships and explains what you are doing to get back on track. You will want to distill that story down to the most important points and never waver from it throughout the negotiation process.

One particularly useful strategy is mentioning that, due to financial hardship, you will soon be meeting with a lawyer who specializes in bankruptcy. This will almost always make creditors more willing to strike a deal as if you file for bankruptcy there is a chance that they will get nothing.

Stay calm: It is important to keep in mind that, no matter what the creditor says, you have the upper hand as the debt you have is leverage over them. Stick to this fact and, no matter what they say, do your best to avoid losing your temper. If you make a scene or cause drama then the creditor will know they are getting to you and will be less willing to make a deal. If you feel yourself losing it, simply tell them that you will call them back and end the call as quickly as possible. If you find the creditor's behavior hard to stomach, simply tell them you are recording the conversation which will put them on their best, and most professional, behavior.

Always ask questions: If the creditor threatens you with a lawsuit or with the loss of property, above all else it is important that you don't let these threats frighten you into making a poor decision. Instead, it is important to ask questions as this will often reveal if the creditor is bluffing or not. For example, if they threaten you with a lawsuit, simply ask when you can expect to be notified of it. Keep notes of these threats as they are often times illegal as creditors are strictly limited as to how they can approach debt, specifically to protect consumers.

Likewise, you are going to want to take notes every time you speak with a creditor including the name of the person you spoke with, the date and the things that were discussed, especially threats. There is typically a statute of limitations as to how long the creditor has to collect on a debt, which varies by region, and they will likely become irater as that time period approaches.

Avoid agreeing to a payment plan: If you agree to a payment plan you will always end up paying more in the long run then if you manage to scrape together a lump sum payment. Depending on the amount you owe, even as little as 30 percent might be enough to satisfy the creditor assuming it is getting close to the end of the timeframe they have to collect on the debt and you have stuck to your story about financial hardship and bankruptcy.

Never be afraid to offer a lowball number, the worst that can happen is that they refuse to take it. If you do end up agreeing to a payment plan make sure you go over your expenses with a fine-tooth comb and ensure you can afford to make the payment every month to avoid finding yourself back in the same situation.

Try and deal with creditors: If you know you are going to be unable to make payments on a debt you have accrued, do your best to come to an agreement with the creditor directly, before the debt is sent to collections. The creditor is always going to be easier to negotiate with than a third-party debt collection service.

Maintaining your credit.

Once you have done the work of repairing your damaged credit score you are going to want to do everything in your power in order to ensure that you don't find yourself back where you started. You have worked diligently to repair the mistakes of the past; don't use it as an excuse to start making new ones. To help keep you on the straight and narrow, consider the following tips.

Always pay your bills on time, all of them: While not every bill that you have will end up on your credit report if you are a few days late when it comes to paying it, you can never know for certain which bills are mission critical and which can be safely ignored until your next pay check. Even a small fine from the local library could ultimately end up on your credit report, dinging your hard-won credit score in the process. Don't take that chance and always remain vigilant when it comes to paying your bills on time.

Avoid using credit cards: While having credit cards improves your credit utilization and credit history, using them too often is a surefire way to start back-sliding, especially if your budget is on the lean side. If you must use your credit cards, take special care to ensure that you never exceed a credit utilization of 30 percent as that's when your credit score will start to take a hit. While going over this limit slightly will only affect your score by a few points, if you are just on the edge of an acceptable score, that might be all it takes to start seeing higher rates as a result.

Pay down your loans: Once you have righted your financial ship, the best way you can keep it on course is to make it a point of paying down your loans as quickly as possible; don't forget, approximately 30 percent of your credit score is influenced by the amount of debt you have which makes it one of the easiest ways to continue improving your score once you are moving in the right direction.

In order to make more money available to pay down your debt, the first thing you are going to want to do is to stop living paycheck to paycheck which means establishing an emergency fund. A solid emergency fund will allow you to live for three months, and pay all your bills, if the worst happens and you find yourself out of the job. Establishing this fund will give you the wiggle room you need to prioritize your debt without worrying about every minor pitfall that comes your way.

Monitor spending: Approximately 40 percent of individuals who find themselves with credit score issues got there simply by not keeping track of their week-to-week spending as well as they should. With the prevalence of online banking, there is no reason why you shouldn't be aware of exactly what your checking account balance is, every minute of every day. Get in the habit of monitoring your spending and you will never be surprised when your bank statement shows up at the end of the month. This doesn't mean you won't want to peruse the statement when it does come in, however, as you never know when a mistake might be made, you never know when a little extra diligence could pay off in a big way.

Remain glued to your credit report: Just because you are out of the woods doesn't mean that nothing new is going to show up on your credit report, whether it is your fault or not. Something new from your past might show up, or one of the bureaus may make a mistake or fail to note the positive changes you have made in a timely manner. The previous chapters have given you tools for dealing with these issues, but you will only be able to put them into action if you are aware of them in the first place. Don't let all your hard work go to waste, continue taking advantage of your free credit report every year.

Chapter 11: How You Can Get Your Credit Reports For Free And How You Should Read Them

It is very important to learn how to find a free copy of your credit reports. For most, they know how they can find a copy of their credit reports for free but you might not. In fact, there are lots of people who have to pay out a lot of money in order to obtain a copy of their reports.

However, you should not be paying out money for credit reports. You are entitled to one free report each and every year.

Obtaining a Free Copy of Your Credit Report

First of all, everyone is entitled to a free credit report. The FCRA – the Fair Credit Reporting Act – is a driving force in which allows every single person to obtain your credit report. The act does ensure that everyone is able to get a copy of their credit report for free.

You can request one credit report only once each year – or every twelve months. One of the easiest ways to view your credit report has to be via the internet. When you view your credit report online, you are able to view it right there and then, instantly, and you are able to choose from three different credit bureaus to view your report.

Experian, Trans Union and Equifax are the three bureaus in which you can obtain your credit report from. So, to obtain your report, you need to fill out some of the basic information on the web, if you choose to go online. You will also need to choose which of the bureaus you wish to receive your credit reports from also.

You usually will be presented with some of the basic questions which you need to fill out. You need to fill out your name, your date of birth, your home address and even your social security number – these are essential in viewing your credit report.

Now, you can ask for a report from one of the three bureaus or all three. This is up to you because it is free of course but it could be much more helpful than one report. It is up to you of course so think carefully; you can get free reports from each of the three credit bureaus so remember that.

If someone asks you to pay don't, you are entitled to a free report each year.

However, if you are using the web to find your credit report, you will need to verify who you are – your identity. Now, this will be basically a few security questions such as about your previous address or even your finances.

The only way to view your credit report will be through verifying your identity, if you cannot o this, you won't get your report. Remember, this step isn't designed to stop you from seeing your report; it's really about protecting you against identity fraud.

Though, once you have verified who you are, you can read your report. Now, interpreting this can be a little tough at times. However, when you use the web, you can scroll down the report and you can find your credit rating.

You will be able to see a lot of information here including what credit is in the past and good or bad and what debts or credits are present. However, there will also be a part of the report that shows your bad credit.

If you have had any late payments then they will be shown on your report and you will easily notice these. That also goes with any repossessions you may have had and collections and foreclosures. These will be represented with some simple icons on the part of your repayment history.

Requesting Your Credit Report by Other Methods

The internet is not just the place in which you can request your credit report for free. There are different methods to so do including by telephone. So if you want to request your credit report via telephone, you will call the credit bureau and request the report.

Your report however will not be given to you over the telephone; it will be mailed out to you via the post. However, you are going to go through a verification process while you use your telephone.

This process will take at least two or three weeks. However, you can also request your report via mail. To do this, you will request by writing to the credit bureaus and fill out your Annual Credit Report Request Form.

Once you fill out the form, you will be able to send this to the credit bureaus. However, even if you have already received a free report, you still may be able to obtain another free report.

First of all, you are able to obtain another free report is you have been out of work for a long period of time but plan to get into employment within two months. This is when you can obtain another free report, however, you can also get another report if your credit application has been denied due to the type of information in which may be contained within your credit report.

You however can also receive your report for free if you are unemployed or received some assistance from the welfare office. If you have been a victim of identity theft or fraud, you are able to get a copy as well.

This is Free:

https://www.creditkarma.com/

Call Experian at 1-888-397-3742 to request a personal credit report.

Call Experian's Business hotline at 1-800-520-1221 for business credit services.

Call Transunion's service at 1-877-322-8228 for personal assistance.

Call 1-800-813-5604 for Transunion's corporate help.

Call 1-800-685-1111 to talk to an agent at Equifax and order a credit report from them.

Call 1-888-202-4025 for the business liaisons at Equifax.

Contact Credit Reporting Agencies to Dispute Information

Obtain your credit report. You will need one to dispute any charge.

Visit the Experian site (see link below) to dispute a charge on your Experian account or call 1-888-397-3742.

You can write to Experian at:

Experian
P.O   Box   9532
Allen, TX 75013

Contact the Transunion dispute center at 1-800-916-8800 or visit them at the ir Web site (see link below).

Write to Transunion at:

Transunion
P.O   Box   6790
Fullerton, CA 92834-6790

Point your browser to the dispute page at the Equifax call 1-800-525-6285 to reach Equifax.

Send snail mail to Equifax:

Equifax
P.O   Box   740241
Atlanta, GA 30374-0241

Remember that you are entitled to getting your credit report from each agency FREE! Once every year you are entitled to this!

How You Can Read Your Credit Report

When you receive your credit report, you are going to be faced with a mountain of information. There is going to be a lot of financial information there and that information can often get you confused and lost but it can seem very difficult to understand everything you face. So, how can you actually read the credit report without finding it difficult?

Well, first and foremost, you are going to see your personal information. This will contain your name, your address and your current and previous employers. Now, you might notice a few mistakes when it comes to the spelling of your name or even your address, but this happens.

You might think that this is something to concern about; however, it isn't actually something too worrying because many reports are filled with minor spelling mistakes. This is because how the credit unions think you spell your name; you spell it a little differently. However, before you actually bypass this part of your report, make sure you are actually reading your own report.

This is very important to do because it might not be your report. Make sure the report is yours. Make sure all of your personal information is current and correct.

Next, you will see your credit summary. This is where you see different credits or accounts you have; so you will see things such as any revolving accounts that amount of total accounts you have and your accounts summary also.

These things might get you a little confused but don't panic too much. This is just summarizing your accounts with your real estate, your mortgages, and loans and any other credit accounts.

Here, you can see the amount of credit account you have currently open and you must ensure that all current accounts that should be opened are. You also need to ensure these are correct as well. You will also be able to see accounts which have been closed and any open accounts also.

There is also a section for you to see about your credit inquiries that you have made over the past two years. You can carefully read through these accounts and see if all are present and correct.

Next, you should see your account history. This is the section which will house your different accounts as well as your account numbers and of course which type of accounts you have opened as well. Here, you should also see information about all of your different loans, your credits and even your payment status.

So let, just say for a moment that you have a mortgage and a car loan as well; you will see the creditors or the lenders name on the report along with the account number. In the report, you will also get to know when the account was opened and the balance that is owed and still owing.

There will be a lot of information here which includes any notes or remarks made by the creditors as well.

This part can be confusing but if you take your time and go through this section carefully, it will be simple in the long run. You can see each of your credits in full which you can check to make sure they are accurate in every piece of information they supply.

If you aren't too sure about something, make a note and continue to check your report. You can come back to something if you aren't too sure later on.

The next part of your credit report will be your public records. Now, this might contain very little information within it but if you have filed for bankruptcy then it will be public knowledge. By this, it means that any creditor or lender can check to see whether you have had a bankruptcy at one point in your life.

This part isn't something to be too concerned about. It can be nothing to worry about at all if you haven't got a bad credit history. If you do then it will be noted down here. It could be anything from bankruptcies to failing to repay your outstanding loans or debt.

The last part you will face will be your credit inquiries. Now, this can be very simple because you can see the creditors who have made an inquiry or two into your credit history. This can be from your bank or even a lender who is thinking about loaning you money. They can of course check the state of your credit before they offer you a loan or even a credit card.

To be honest, a credit report might seem to be very scary at times, although, it can be very simple to understand. Once you know what your credit report contains, and how you should tackle reading it, it is actually very simple.

You do not need to panic any more when you wish to read your credit report. It can be very simple and easy to do so even if you haven't read a credit report before. Even if you have just requested your very first credit report, you can still easily read it and understand what it all means.

Remember, understanding your credit reports can be very important no matter who you are. You want to be able to read your reports correctly so that there are no mistakes. What is more, you also want to be able to read your reports correctly so that if there are any mistakes or errors, you can pick them up and dispute them as soon as you notice them. These can all help in determining whether you have good or bad credit.

Chapter 12: Disputing To All 3 Major

Credit Bureaus

In this section I will provide you with sample dispute letters, explain how the dispute process works and show you how to get your dispute settled on the first try.

The dispute process was, at one time, rather simple before technology took over. Before, you could send in a dispute letter and someone working at the bureau would actually handle the dispute. This means that when your dispute letter was received an actual person would pick up the phone and call the creditor to verify the debt. Unfortunately, that was in the good ole days!

Now when you send in a letter **e-Oscar** takes the dispute. The computer program e-Oscar (Online Solution for Complete and Accurate Reporting) breaks the dispute down into a 2-3 digit code, then asks the creditor to verify the code instead of asking to verify the actual information.

This is the main contributing factor to how invalid items still show on a report even though a previous dispute was submitted and validated.

Just for the record … I am Not a fan of Oscar!

The reason behind the bureaus using e-Oscar is to process disputes faster but the results are often inaccurate. Basically, they failed us as consumers to investigate our disputes because no one person is actually investigating on our behalf. The key factor to getting your dispute handled by an individual rather than a computer is simple … **bypass** e-Oscar. This can be done through simple tricks when submitting your dispute.

Items that will be needed to submit your dispute:

*Your Credit Report

*Any supporting documentation that you have. (Receipts or proof of age of account for example)

*A copy of your Drivers License or ID with correct mailing address (if the address on your ID card is incorrect then you must include proof of address. This can be done with a utility bill or any other form of mail)

*A copy of your Social Security Card

*Your dispute letter

Trick #1 to Bypass e-Oscar

The type and color of paper you use.

When your dispute letter arrives at the credit Bureau it will be loaded into e-Oscar. The key here is to make sure that e-Oscar is unable to read your letter and supporting documentation. Use a bright florescent colored paper or if your printer is capable use a card stock paper. This will usually make the system unable to recognize the documentation. Then it has to be handed over to an individual for investigation.

Trick #2 to Bypass e-Oscar

Always handwrite your letters.

If for some reason the paper is not enough to kick it out of the system this is almost a guarantee to work. E-Oscar scans the document and tries to pick up on key words to decide how to handle your dispute. In most cases, it will be unable to read your handwriting even if it is perfect.

Trick #3 to Bypass e-Oscar

Lots and Lots of Staples

According to the list I gave you previously, you should have at least 2-3 pieces of paper in your dispute when sent to the Bureaus. Your dispute letter, a copy of Id, and a copy of your Social Security Card. Go staple happy! I can assure you that who ever is loading the information into e-Oscar is not going to stand there to remove your mountain of staples. It will be passed over into the investigate stack.

Make sure you use all 3 of these tricks at the same time when submitting your dispute. It will get your claim read and investigated every time. By law, the Bureau has 30 days to investigate your dispute. They will notify you in writing with their investigation results and provide you an updated report showing where the changes were made.

Writing the Dispute Letter

Your dispute letter does not have to be anything fancy. It can be long and drawn out or quick and to the point. I have provided you will some example letters that you are welcome to use. Remember, however, they MUST be handwritten.

Make sure you put the date on your letter and include whichever Bureaus you are disputing in the heading. State clearly in your letter the reason for your dispute. Also, clearly state which accounts your disputing. On your credit report, locate the item that is in question. Make note on the letter of the creditor name and account number. Sometimes only partial account numbers will be shown. Make sure to include as much of the account number that is available to you. Also, you will want to notate any balances and any dates of reporting that are offered.

Always end the letter with your signature. Below your signature be sure to print your name, date of birth and Social Security number. Attached to the letter you will be providing proof of the items in your signature section. (With lots of staples)

Sample letter 1 – Inaccurate Information Dispute

To: Name of Credit Bureau

NameDate

Address

This letter is to inform you that you are reporting inaccurate credit information on my report.

I am upset that the following information is on my credit report:

[Name of Account and account #]

Reason for inaccuracy (the amount is incorrect, dates of collection are incorrect, duplicate collection) make sure and state the reason you believe the account to be inaccurate

These inaccurate items are embarrassing! They are preventing me from obtaining the credit I deserve. As I am sure you are aware, there are laws that ensure that credit bureaus report only accurate credit information. It is evident that the inclusion of this inaccurate information is a mistake on either your part or the reporting creditor's part.

It is with great concern that I insist you verify that this information as incorrect and delete it from my profile. Due to the damaging effects of such negative inaccurate information I must insist that this is done immediately.

Regards,

Name

SS#

DOB

Sample #2 – Statue of Limitations Dispute

To: Name of Credit Bureau

NameDate

Address

This letter is to inform you that you are reporting illegal information on my credit profile. As I am sure you are aware, the law states that there is a _____year Statue Of Limitations (the number of years depends on your state law) This account has exceeded that specified amount of time.

It is with great concern that I insist you delete it from my profile. Due to the damaging effects of such negative information I must insist that this is done immediately.

I am upset that the following information is on my credit report:

1. [Name of Account and account #]

Regards,

Name

SS#

DOB

Sample #3 – Licensing Dispute

To: Name of Credit Bureau

NameDate

Address

This letter is to inform you that you are reporting illegal information on my credit profile. As I am sure you are aware, all companies must hold a valid business license. The creditor listed below has a business license that is no longer valid. Therefore this collection is invalid.

It is with great concern that I insist you delete it from my profile. Due to the damaging effects of such negative information I must insist that this is done immediately.

Here is the information on the collection of concern:

1. [Name of Account and account #] include any proof you may have that the license is invalid.

Regards,

Name

SS#

DOB

Sample #4 – Debt Validation Dispute

If at any point you get an account verified by the Bureau always ask them for Debt Validation (you may find other inaccuracies that will allow you to have it removed)

To: Name of Credit Bureau

NameDate

Address

Recently I submitted a request to have an account removed from my report. In your investigation results it stated that you had verified the information for that account and that it was a valid account.

Please provide me with any information that was obtained for this validation during this investigation. I am positive that there has been a mistake made here and I am eager to have this removed.

Here is the account that is in question:

1. [Name of Account and account #]

Regards,

Name

SS#

DOB

Chapter 13: Actions For Credit Health And

Credit Repair

The following are five specific suggestions for protecting your credit score.

(1)Avoid offers for instant credit and new lines of credit

"How would you like to save 10% on your purchases today?" We've all been asked that question when purchasing items in stores. Every store under the sun would like to offer you their own credit card, because it is lucrative for their bottom line. However this will not be good for you credit score. The damage to your score you will incur by opening a new line of credit with a retail store is not worth the few dollars you might save. Department store credit is poor quality credit and the credit scoring system generally frowns upon it.

Just don't apply for a new credit card through a store. You may want or need to apply for a new car loan, a new home loan or a home loan refinancing. By applying for a store credit to save a few dollars, you could be hurting your chance for an important loan at a good rate for many months while the credit scoring system is evaluating your activity under your new credit card.

(2)Avoid overspending

Spending affects credit. Thirty percent of your credit score is made up of how you manage your debt, and when your credit card balances exceed 30% of their available limit, the credit scoring system flags you and your score goes down instantly. The logic behind this is that if you suddenly max out your credit cards, it looks to the system as though you are in financial trouble. A good rule is to charge only if you can pay the balance in full on the next statement date. Overspending and overcharging will also cause you to carry larger balances longer, resulting in more interest and penalty payments. It is best to keep you balances low at all times.

(3)Pay your bills on time

Payment history is 35% of your credit score. One payment 30 days late can cost you 50 points on your score. December is traditionally the busiest time of the year. Active calendars filled with work and social commitments for family and friends and the frenzy of the season can preoccupy you and cause you to be late in paying your bills. Make staying on top of your bill payment a priority. Keep all of your bills in a file and make sure you pay them on time. By doing so you will save points on your credit score and avoid those ridiculous late charges of $39 or more.

Additionally, when you are late in paying your bills, you nullify any preferential finance rate in your contract and your account will probably default to a dramatically higher interest rate. So: (1) a ding to your credit score, (2) a high late fee, and (3) a huge increase in interest rates are all big incentives to make sure you are on time with paying your bills. Recent real-world examples have shown people being hit with 30% annual interest rates by being late on only one payment in their credit account. If you carry a large credit card debt, this can literally cost you thousands of dollars!

(4)Plan and prepare your gift giving

We all do it. You walk into a store ready to buy a specific item and end up getting lured into a spending vortex. Panic spending occurs because the store does not have the item you went in to buy or deciding that if you but this item for this person, then you have to buy this item for another person. You succumb to the temptation of the latest must-have gadget. You can prevent this well-woven retailer trap by doing your research on line. By preparing before you enter the doorstep of the alluring retail establishment, you determine where you can purchase specific items and for what price. By doing so you can avoid the retail traps and retain control of your spending and your sanity.

Online shopping sites have grown tremendously and are now the norm, with traffic to those sites growing continuously at 30+% per year. There is a wealth of information on the web and it is now easy to find the hottest items and where to get them. In almost all cases website buying will be done by credit card. Just be sure you pay your credit card bill within the payment time period, and it will help strengthen your credit score.

(5)Manage your credit wisely

You should keep track of your credit card balances and keep them as low as possible. Studies show that as consumers increase their credit card balances, they become increasingly apathetic about their balances and even about adding new debt. By tracking balances you will maintain a sense of control over your credit score and your finances. It is helpful to write out a chart, or make a spreadsheet showing to whom you owe, how much you owe and what the minimum payment is.

It will help you to get a handle on your bills and help start planning how to pay them off. Most people who have credit cards can live within their means if they plan wisely for spending on what they need and what they want, and schedule purchases to fit their cash availability and credit scheduling.

The following are actions you can take to help repair your credit.

If your credit score is inaccurate or lower than you think it should be, there are certain actions you can take to initiate repair. The credit bureaus provide dispute phone numbers and procedures to follow if you dispute some information on your report. Although these procedures are very specific, it does not hurt your credit rating to initiate a dispute because the credit bureaus want to insure that the information in their databases is accurate and correct. You should remember that the credit bureaus have nothing against you personally; they are strictly reporting information available to determine your credit score.

It is possible to hire companies that will take some hassle out of attempting credit repair. But they require you to provide a lot of information and, by the time you have done that, you might as well do the same job yourself for little or no cost.

(1)Obtain your credit reports

You are entitled by law to receive a free copy of your credit report from the three credit bureaus once each year. The bureaus will charge a fee to provide more frequent copies. It is also possible to purchase a combined report showing all three credit scores (try google searching for credit repair on line).

You should obtain all three reports because some lenders do not report data to all three bureaus, but maybe to only one. There is no required consistency in lender reporting.

(2)Analyze your credit reports

You should carefully examine all of your credit reports. The reports from the three bureaus will look similar but may contain some different data due to differences in lender reporting. The reports will list both your "private" credit transactions and data from "public records" such as bankruptcy filings.

In your search, look for (a) incorrect or false information; (b) information on any of your accounts that are listed as over the limit; (c) Information on your accounts that show "past due" or "in collection." If you disagree with any of these items, you should file a dispute to the bureau that is reporting it.

You will receive instructions and procedures from the bureaus on how to dispute credit reporting information. Specific procedures can be carried out via mail, phone or on the Internet. Detailed dispute information sent by mail has advantages because you can send photocopies of records, receipts and cancelled checks, which support your case.

You must have sufficient information to convince the credit bureau that you have a good case for credit repair. You can't just send a letter saying, "I'm disputing this overdue report because I made the payment on time. Honest!" You need to support your case with cancelled checks, receipts or payment source documents.

If you initiate a dispute, the credit bureau must respond to you with a reasonable time, such as 45 days. If your dispute is successful the credit bureau will issue an updated report and also notify the other credit agencies of the correction.

(3)Take repair corrective action

Since your payment history is the most important factor in your credit report (worth 35%), a history of "past due" accounts will have a significant effect on your overall score. You should investigate these and make sure erroneous data are corrected. The goal is to have "past due" accounts reported as "paid off" or "current."

If you have an account listed as "charged off," it means it is more than 180 days overdue, and this is the worst status you can possible have. You can fix this problem by paying off the account in full before the 180 day limit. This may be difficult to do, but the last thing you want is a "charged off" account on your credit report. Do everything possible to repair a "charged off" account. Once it is paid off it is reported as paid with zero balance.

Chapter 14: Student Loan Relief Programs

We are in a though economy and people are having a harder time than ever to pay back their student loan debt. Many Americans are working two jobs just to make ends meet and a number of young graduates are finding it hard to find a job in their field of study.

What should you do if you are finding hard to make your student loan payments?

Student loans can be a good way to build an excellent credit score; it is viewed as an instalment account or trade line on your credit because of the fixed payment amount, so you should do everything possible not to have a late payment on your student loans. If are having financial troubles, you may be eligible for a deferment or forbearance on your federal student loans. This will allow you to temporarily postpone or reduce your monthly payments and help you avoid going into default on your student loans

Deferment is a period during which repayment of the principal and interest of your loan is temporary delayed. Qualifying for deferment can be granted under s circumstances such as unemployed, minimum income, or serving in the army or community. You must contact the financial aid office at the school you are attending as well as your lender. They will give you the documentation necessary to complete your deferment request.

Forbearance is when you are granted permission by your lender to stop making payments or to lower your monthly payments on your federal student loans for up to 12 months. This is an option if you don't qualify for a deferment but with a forbearance, interest will accrue on your subsidized and unsubsidized loans. Mandatory forbearances maybe given for:

Serving in a medical or dental internship or residency program.

The total amount you owe each month for all student loans you received is 20% or more of your total monthly gross income.

National service position for which you received a national service award.

Teaching service that would qualify for teacher loan forgiveness.

You qualify for partial repayment of your loans under the U.S. Department Of Defence Student Loan Repayment Program.

You are a member of the National Guard and have been activated by governor, but you are not are not eligible for a military deferment

Deferments are a better choice than forbearance on your federal student loans because of the interest paid by the government. Forbearance is the second best option topostponing your payments. Until you have been approved for a deferment or forbearance you must continue paying your student loans unless instructed otherwise. Your credit will not be affected in these two options and it will continue to give you a good credit history.

PAYE Program

The Pay As You Earn program is a federal program that was passed into law on December of 2012. It was the first student debt relief law signed by President Barack Obama. Student loan borrowers must have loans that were taken out after October 1, 2007, and must have received at least one disbursement after October 1, 2011. Also, the standard 10-year repayment amount must exceed 10 percent of the borrower's discretionary income.

Program advantages

• The program keep payments low in the early years of the loan, then raise to track salary increase.

• After 20 years of payments there will be loan forgiveness.

Some borrowers who choose to enter public service will see their balance forgiven in only 10 years.

The government pays unpaid accrued interest on Direct Subsidized Loans and on the subsidized portion of Direct Consolidation Loans for three years if your payment amount does not cover the interest. Also, interest capitalization is limited, even in deferment and forbearance for as long as the borrower meets the hardship requirements.

Program disadvantages

They will look at debt compared to salary so eligibility and payment caps are tied to household income, not individual income. For a married borrower, whose spouse earns around the same income but has no outstanding student loans, might not benefit at all.

The borrower may have to pay income tax on the forgiven portion of the loan immediately on the forgiven amount. You need to save that amount for that tax payment.

Participants must provide qualifying documentation annually

Borrowers who participate will pay more interest overall, due to the lengthening of the loan repayment period.

This program applies to federal loans only. Federal Direct Loans, although other student loans are taken into account when determining hardship. Federal Family Education Loans or (FFEL) loans are not eligible for this plan, but they will be considered when eligibility is determined. FFELs are eligible for Income-Based Repayment plans.

Keep in mind, if the amount is larger enough to last up to 20 years the total amount will not change no matter the size of the loan.

REPAYE Program

President Obama recent issued a memorandum for an expansion of the PAYE Program to 5 million more borrowers. The Revised Pay As You Earn Program or (REPAYE) maybe available late 2015 or early 2016. Revision that has been made to REPAYE will include lower income borrows but limit high income borrows who may try to take advantage of these generous payment terms.

Program advantages

The program will be open to all borrowers with Federal Direct Loans, no matter the period of the initial loan date.

Borrows with older loans can be consolidated to become eligible.

No income requirements

No Financial Hardship proof required

The program payments equal 10% of the borrows' discretionary income.

Loan forgiveness in 20 years for Undergraduates

Loan forgiveness in 25 years for Graduates

The program limits the interest charged to the borrowers when the payment when the payment amount don't cover the months' interest. The borrower will only get charged for 50% of the interest that month and the Government will pay for the remaining interest the borrows'.

Program disadvantages

They will look at debt compared to salary so eligibility and payment caps are tied to household income, not individual income. For a married borrower, whose spouse earns around the same income but has no outstanding student loans, might not benefit at all.

The borrower may have to pay income tax on the forgiven portion of the loan immediately on the forgiven amount. You need to save that amount for that tax payment.

There is no cap on the amount that the payment can increase to when the borrows' income raises.

You must Re-Certify you household income and family size or be place in a in an "Alternate Plan".

Income-Based repayment options

Income-Based Repayment (IBR) plans are available, and are based on 15 percent of the borrows' discretionary income. There are other repayment options that can extent repayment plans and graduated repayment plans, in which payments start low but increase every two years for up to 25 years to keep the payments affordable. FFELs are not eligible for this program but borrowers can consolidate FFELs into the

Direct Loan program. The loan must have been initiated after October 1, 2007.

Relief For Student Loans That Are In Default

We discussed in early chapters how student loan defaults can ruin your financial future. Some of you reading this book are already in this position but there is hope. Two main options for federal student loans in default which are loan rehabilitation and loan consolidation.

Loan rehabilitation program

This program requires the borrower in default to make voluntary on-time payments. These payments are based on the borrowers' income versus their expenses. The borrower must make nine monthly payments within 20 days of the due date during the 10 month consecutive period. Once the borrower has successfully completed the consecutive payment schedule the loan will come out of default. The lender will use the IBR formula for older loans and on the borrower making student loan payments of 15% of disposable income. This does not mean that you are eligible for IBR while you are still in default. Instead, the loan holder will use the 15% IBR formula to determine a reasonable and affordable payment amount. If you successfully rehabilitate the loan, you can then request an income-driven repayment plan.

Program advantages

You no longer will be in default status by your lender on your credit report.

No more garnishments of your wages.

Them will stop taking you income tax returns

You will be eligible to receive federal student loans and federal grants again.

You can quality again for a HUD and VA loans

Please keep in mind that you are entitled to get out of default through rehabilitation only once per loan. Student loans you have rehabilitated before August 14, 2008 and go back into default on that loan, you can still rehabilitate again but this is subject to the one-time limit.

There are also collection fees paid to the collection agencies. As of July 1, 2014, this should be no more than 16% of the unpaid principal and accrued interest at the time of the sale of the loan.

Loan consolidation program

This is involves making voluntary on-time payments the borrowers' income versus their expenses for three consecutive reasonable and affordable monthly payments or agree to pay under the Income Contingent Repayment (ICRP) or Income Based Repayment (IBR) plan. This is the quickest way but credit will not be restored and you will still owe collections fees that can increase your debt up to 25%.

Chapter 15: Understanding Your Credit

Report

Your credit report is not all that easy to understand. There are a lot of different categories in the report and that means you need to weigh out different things in order to make sure that your credit score is going to be high enough for you to get the things you want.

The best scores are those that are over 900 but not many people are actually able to achieve that. If your score is over a 700 you actually have really good credit and you're pretty much guaranteed any type of credit that you might apply for. But you want to keep in mind that different types of credit card companies or credit agencies will want a different score.

If your score is in the 600's you have a decent chance of getting credit in most places but not all. This isn't guaranteed however. There are plenty of agencies that will consider you a little bit of a risk.

Your credit score is actually an indication of how much of a risk it is to give you credit. When you first start out getting credit you have a low credit score. This tells the person checking your score that there is a high level of risk involved. They don't know if you're going to pay the bills or if you're going to rack up high amounts of charges. That's why your score is low. As you get more recorded payments your score will go up because the risk of you not paying for things is getting lower.

Now it's not just late payments or missed payments that are going to count against you in regards to your credit score. There are actually a lot of different factors that cause problems with your credit score (or improve your credit score)

So let's break them down a little and look at what's on your credit report.

Public records are one of the first things that show up on your credit report. These are the worst things you can have, judgments and tax liens against you. Any of these are going to make a big dent in your credit score and they're going to continue to work against you for a very long time (up to 7 years). You definitely don't want these if you can help it.

The next thing is going to be your credit items. These are credit cards, loans, mortgages and any other credit account that you've had in the past. Most accounts that are considered old (closed more than 10 years ago) will not report unless you've had a collection filed for that account.

Each of your credit items is going to count towards your credit score. Every on time payment is going to count in your favor and every late payment, missed payment or collection is going to count against you. Each balance is going to be reported as well and high balances are also going to count against you.

Remember we said before that you want to have a high available credit balance but you also want to have a low balance on the credit you're using. What the credit reporting agency does is look at how much you're able to spend on all of your credit cards and add that together. That's your available credit balance. They then look at how much money you owe on each of those cards and add that all together.

The amount owed is divided by the amount available and that's your total balance percentage. You want to keep this percentage low because that reflects well on your credit card. A high percentage is going to look bad and lower your credit score.

The total amount of accounts that you have as well as the types of accounts is going to count towards your score as well. You actually want to have a moderate number of accounts (more than 10) as long as you can keep them all current. You also want to have an assortment of accounts (credit cards, mortgages, car loans, student loans, etc.) this is going to improve your score as well.

Finally, the number of inquiries that you have will affect your score. You want to cut down on the amount of inquiries that you have because every one is a slight ding to your account. What these are is every time that you apply for credit. If you apply they check your credit score and when they check your credit score it goes down a little bit. These inquiries stay on your credit report for some time as well.

That's why you want to apply for credit infrequently and only if you're sure you're going to get it. Getting the credit will help improve your score more than it's going to hurt for the inquiry.

So all in all you want to make sure of a few important things in regards to your credit report:

Have several different accounts (10 or more)

Keep all accounts current

Avoid public records

Have a variety of types of accounts (loans and credit cards)

Keep your available balance high

Keep the balance in use low

Don't apply for credit unless necessary

Never apply for credit unless you're sure you'll be approved

Dispute accounts that aren't correct

Make payments on any past due accounts and pay off collections

By doing all of these things your credit score will actually increase over time. It will take some time and you're definitely going to need to work at it but you'll be able to bring your credit score back up. Once you're able to bring your score back up you'll find it even easier to get out of debt and you'll start saving better as well.

The reason your credit score is going to affect this is because your credit score actually has a lot to do with you getting approved for everything from credit cards to car loans to housing. It also has to do with the interest rates that you're given. As your score goes up you'll be able to request lower interest rates and that makes it even easier to pay off debts and stay out of debt in the long run. Staying out of debt means you have more money to put away towards your savings. So it's really a win all the way around.

Chapter 16: Increase Credit Limit With

Poor Credit

A lot of the advice about increasing your credit limit seems to be geared toward people who already have good credit score. But what if you have poor credit? **Is it still possible to increase your credit limit?** The answer is yes. However, it's a little harder, and may take a little bit more time.

First, you need to understand why your credit is poor. For some people, they don't have much of a credit history. Since creditors simply don't know if they are credit-worthy or not, they won't be looking to increase their limit. For this, the best thing is time. As you show you will be paying off your bills and being responsible, your score will go up, and you will be more trustworthy. You could also get a secured credit card, as a way to build up more credit in a shorter amount of time.

For other people, they may be coming up close against their balance, which will give them poor credit and make creditors leery about extending them anymore. There is no magic formula here, you simply have to work on lowering your balance. Once you get the credit utilization rate down to a more manageable level, you will have the opportunity to increase your credit limit.

Still other people have poor credit because they are not always good about paying your bills. If you miss payments, that is a good way to have your credit score take a big hit. Also, if you miss payments at your current credit level, there will be no rush to grant you an increase. Here, you simply need to stay on top of all of your payments and make sure they are getting paid on time.

If you have poor credit, it is still possible to increase your credit limit. It will take a little more time and persistence, and might require a little extra hard work from you, but it can be done.

HOW MUCH OF A CREDIT LIMIT INCREASE SHOULD YOU ASK FOR?

If you have decided that you should try to increase your credit limit, and you know how to do it, it still brings up one more question – **how much of a credit limit increase should you ask for?**

You don't want to ask for too little, because then you may be missing out on the upside of the increase. However, you don't want to ask for too much, because that might cause them not to give you anything at all.

Unfortunately, there is no hard and fast rule. However, there are some guidelines to use.

One general guideline is to ask for about 10-25% of your current limit. If this is your first time asking for an increase, I would try to stick at about the 25% range, because that will give you a nice bump, but will also seem very reasonable to the creditor.

If you have had the card a long time and have had multiple increases, I think it would be reasonable to ask for double your current limit. I don't know that they would give you that much, but they would at least be able to give you some type of counter offer.

HOW LONG SHOULD YOU WAIT TO INCREASE YOUR CREDIT LIMIT?

Once you get a new credit card, you might be wondering how long you should have the card until you try and **increase the credit limit**. If it is lower than you would have liked, you might want to increase as soon as possible.

However, it is usually recommended that you wait at least six months after you get the card to request and increase to your credit limit. That way, you can build up time to be seen as trustworthy by the credit card company, and build up a history or making payments on time.

Of course, this comes with the caveat that you still should not request an increase if you are going to soon be making a big purchase or applying for a big loan. That is because it could cause a short-term dip to your score, and you'll want to be sure to request an increase well before you try to get that big loan.

So, if you get a new card, wait at least six months to request an increase to your credit limit. That should be enough time for you to build up a strong profile with the company so that they will trust you, and grant you that increase.

Chapter 17: Paying Bills

I Started Paying ALL Of My Bills On Time

And, if at all possible, in full each month – I cannot emphasize enough how important this particular step was for me. It's probably one of the most important things that one can do to improve credit rating and maintain a healthy credit report.

I'm referring to ALL types of bills – rent or mortgage, gas bill, water and power, cell phone, cable or satellite, internet, credit cards, loans, doctor's bills, tuition fees, etc. **I made sure to pay any statement or bill that I received for anything at all on time**.

If I couldn't afford to pay them on time? Then it was time to cut back on what I was spending.

By paying my bills on time, I can avoid late charges and penalties saving me hundreds of dollars over time. A late fee for a credit card bill can be as much as $35! That's a stiff penalty to pay for being even one day late on a bill.

Just one late payment on any of the monthly bills can lower your FICO score significantly. According to myFICO: Making your credit payments on time is one of the biggest contributing factors to your credit score.

Payment history contributes to approximately 35% of your FICO score!

One rule of thumb, which I use, is **not to buy anything that I cannot afford to pay in full when the bill comes**. Buying a home or getting a car loan can be an exception of course.

I really needed reminders for making my payments on time, and I set up automatic reminders or automatic payments for each of my bills. I rarely need to log into accounts to pay bills now, and I don't remember the last time that I wrote a check to send in the mail for bill. I keep any paper bills or statements that I receive in one place, and I check this place at least weekly. Don't lose track of the bills that come in!

My credit card bills are automatically set to be paid from my checking out in full each month. I know my payments will never be late, and I never carry balances over to the next month thus avoiding hefty interest charges.

I'm going to include information here about collection accounts as well. Accounts that are not paid in a timely manner are sent to a collection agency that will try to collect the amount owed. Collection agencies are hired to recoup as much of the amount owed as possible and they use many tactics to scare people into paying them. Items that have been sent to a collection agency are considered a negative or derogative item on a credit report and lower the FICO score quite a bit.

Paying off accounts that have been sent to a collection agency is something that some people don't want to do and wind up just ignoring those accounts (and constant calls from the collection agencies).

My recommendation is to pay off any accounts in collection if at all possible. Here's my experience:

Collection items will stay on a credit report for seven years before they are supposed to be removed. And after seven years, it's not guaranteed that they will be removed because one collection agency can sell your account to another and then that collection item is listed again on your credit report as a new negative item.

This shouldn't happen, but it does. It happened to me. And trying to communicate with the collection agency about the new delinquency date can be an arduous process.

Seven years (or more) is a long time to wait and see if a negative item will be removed. And if it's not removed, that negative item stays on your credit report for at least another seven years.

I wanted to avoid this energy drain. I called the collection company and did my best to come up with a payment plan to clear my debt. They will sometimes accept a lower payment as payment in full and then list the account as a "charge off." While charge offs are considered a negative item on my credit history, the debt was taken care of and I was on my way to peace of mind and better credit in the long run.

Remember that school loan that my father had included in his bankruptcy? It went into collections when the bankruptcy was reversed and immediately went onto my credit report as a negative item.

I arranged payments with the collection agency and asked them if they would remove the item from my credit report. I explained my situation in a very nice way, and the representative said that he would see what he could do. I wasn't expecting anything knowing how collection agencies are, but the item was removed from my credit report because I was making payments towards the balance. You never know what kind of arrangement can be made with the collection agencies. Ask for

what you want in a friendly way and see
what happens.

Chapter 18: Dealing With Your Credit

Report To Deal With Your Credit Score

If you want to improve your credit score, you need to go right to the source - your credit report. Your credit report contains the information and data on which your credit score is based. If you can alter or update the information in your credit report, your credit score will change to reflect the alterations. For this reason, getting and checking you credit report is one of the first things you should do when you attempt to repair your credit score. There are a few tips that can help you deal with your credit report so that you can give your credit score a boost:

Tip #19: Dispute errors on your credit report Contact each of the three major credit bureaus - TransUnion, Equifax, and Experian - and get copies of your credit reports and credit scores. Carefully read over the reports and note any errors. In writing, contact the credit bureaus and ask that mistakes be removed or investigated.

This is called a dispute letter and once it is received, credit bureaus have to investigate your dispute within thirty days of receiving your letter. It is important to keep a copy of your letter and it is important to note the date the letter was sent. You should not be accusatory or abusive in your letter - calmly and clearly state the problem and request an investigation.

Note that you are aware the agency is required to investigate the claim within thirty days and note that you will follow up. Be sure that you do follow up with the issues you raised in your letter - just because the agency investigates does not always mean that your credit report will end up error-free.

Many credit bureaus now make it possible for you to correct errors on your credit report online - and many have information on their web sites that tells you exactly how disputes must be handled to be effectively removed. It is important that you follow this information exactly so that the inaccuracies on your credit report are removed promptly and your credit score is updated as soon as possible. Tip #20: Add a note to your credit report if there is a problem you can't resolve Sometimes, there are legitimate reasons why you didn't pay a bill. If a contractor refused to finish a job or did a poor job, then you may have refused payment, but the non-payment may still count against you on your credit report. If there are any unusual circumstances surrounding your credit report that may affect your credit rating - such as a case of identity theft - you can ask that a note be attached to your credit report to explain the problem.

Some lenders will pay attention to this and some will not, but it is a better solution than nothing at all. Such a note will not affect your credit score but will affect your credit report. More importantly, it leaves a paper trail of the problem that lenders can look at if they choose.

Tip #21: Make sure you know who is looking at your credit report and why Many inquiries look bad on your credit report, but more than that you likely want to know who can see your personal financial information, now that you know that your personal information is stored in a credit report. If you sign a document with a lender or apply for credit online, you can be sure that someone is looking at your credit report.

However, you may want to look over other documents in order to see who is taking a peek. Insurance agents will often look at your credit report, for example. Some landlords and potential employers will, too. You need to be careful about online sources, too. In general, when you provide someone with your social insurance number, you may be giving permission to look at your credit report. You shouldn't bar people from looking, but knowing who is looking is good financial practice.

Tip #22: Know the difference between soft and hard inquiries

When you pull your credit report to look at it, it is counted as a "soft inquiry." Only "hard inquiries" from lenders will affect your credit score dramatically. Although checking your credit score too often is an expensive habit, you should not avoid checking your credit report because you fear it will make your credit rating worse.

Tip #23: Contact creditors as well as credit bureaus when correcting inaccuracies in your credit report When debtors find mistakes on their credit report, they often only contact the credit bureaus. While this is the most effective way to resolve the issue, you should in some cases contact the creditors whose account has caused a ding on your credit report. This can help future dings and resolve problems faster.

Consider an example: Let's say that you were late sending a credit card payment two months ago because you were sick. The late payment is listed as a ding on your credit report even though you have paid it already. You should contact the credit bureau in order to get the error removed.

However, if you notice that the same credit card company has you listed as having late payments three months when you paid on time, then it is time to contact the credit company and ask how to resolve the problem.

The information reported about you to credit bureaus should be accurate - if it is not, then the credit company should work to make sure that they correct the problem so that it does not happen again. You have an advantage in this - the credit company, unlike the credit bureau, depends on your business for their money.

This means that the credit company (or any other bill company presenting inaccurate information about you) is well motivated to correct the problem or risk losing you as a client.

If you find that a company consistently reports inaccurate information about you to credit bureaus, consider making a formal complaint to the company about it or switch companies. There is no reason why one company's poor organization should cost you your good credit score.

Tip #24: Look out where you get your credit report - and what it contains You can get your credit score from any number of resources. One place you can get it from is from credit bureaus themselves. You can pay for the service, but you qualify for one free credit report a year or qualify for a free credit report if you have recently been turned down for credit or if you think you may have been the victim of identity theft.

If you can, get a copy of your free credit report from each of the three major credit bureaus. If

you can't get a free credit report, you should still try to get one, even if costs a few dollars. The savings you will enjoy on your loan rates when you improve your credit score will more than pay for the cost of the reports.

There are a number of online companies that offer free online credit reports. These offers are very attractive because you get an online report without having to wait for a report to be sent to you, and you often can get several reports from the different credit bureaus at once, which can save you time.

However, these online companies vary widely, so you will want to compare a few different firms before choosing one. You will also need to read the online company's agreement very carefully - some promise free credit reports only with the purchase of a credit repair program or some other kit. In some cases, you can decline the offer and still get the report but in other cases you cannot.

Buyer beware.

Also, some companies will offer you free credit reports that are really a combination of reports from the three major credit bureaus. This is not useful, since you will want to compare each of the three credit bureau reports and fix each credit score separately. You will want to look out for online companies that offer credit reports that are very condensed and you will want to avoid companies that will spam you (send you unsolicited emails) trying to get you to subscribe to some service. Always read carefully to see whether the free credit report offer is legitimate.

That said, there are a number of online companies that offer credit reports and credit scores at no charge and these can be a useful way for you to start your credit repair, especially if you are comfortable around computers.

If you don't qualify for a free credit report from the credit bureaus, a legitimate online company may be your best bet of getting your credit information so that you can start repairing your credit risk rating.

You do qualify for one free credit report per year. You can get this credit report through email at www.annualcreditreport.com or by calling 877-322-8228.

You can also ask for your free credit report by mail by sending a letter to Annual Credit Report Request Service, P.O. Box 105281, Atlanta, GA 30348_5281 or by filling out the form available at the Federal Trade Commission's Web site at: http://www.ftc.gov/bcp/conline/edcams/credit/docs/fact_act_request_form.pdf.

No matter where you get your credit score and credit report, make sure that you get the most complete information package you can. Credit reports are not very exciting or even easy to read. If you are ordering your report online, look for one that includes graphs or lots of details that are easy to understand.

Make sure that you get both your credit report and your credit score - even if you have to pay extra. If you get just your report, you will not be able to follow the secret and complicated math formulas used to arrive at your score and the report itself will not make as much financial sense to you if you don't have your score in front of you, as well.

When you do get your credit report you will notice that it contains lots if information about you, including:

1) Your personal and contact information. This will include your name and your address, as well as your past several addresses, your social insurance number, your employers (past and present) and your birth date.

2) Your personal information about credit. A credit report notes all the details of your loans, including the types of loans you have now and have recently had, the dates these loans were opened, the credit limit on each loan, how well you have been repaying those loans (this is important - skipped or late payments count heavily against you in your credit score), and who your lenders are.

3) Information about you that is on the public record. This may include bankruptcies, unpaid taxes, unpaid child support, tax liens, your dealings with collection agencies, foreclosures, loan defaults, civil lawsuits that you have been

involved in, and other information. Much of this will stay on your credit report and will seriously affect your credit score.

4) Information about who has looked at your credit report and credit score. Every time that someone looks at your credit score it is called an "inquiry." Your credit report lists who has looked at your credit report in the past two years and how often you have applied for loans and credit in that period of time. Too many inquiries tends to look bad and tends to affect your credit score.

When you get your credit report, it is important that you look at all parts of your credit report and understand what you are reading. Mistakes in any area of your credit report can affect your score, so be sure to check the entire report for inaccuracies and errors.

Chapter 19: Pros & Cons Of Credit Repair

Services

Once you have cleared your credit report from any errors and the score it is still not up to par to what you want, then you may require the services of credit repair agencies. These agencies have experience in cleaning up your history, delinquencies, charge offs and other negative information in your report. They will make also make disputes on your behalf.

Most of these credit repair agencies work on loopholes in the rules that determine your report and score. For example, if the agency did not verify or used improper means to verify the data they received from their source, then it can be a cause for dispute. The credit bureau usually uses automated software to make the verification but actual calls are still required. If they cannot provide proof of the call, then it can be a cause for dispute.

Legitimate credit repair agencies do not claim that by employing them, they will guarantee a significant increase in your credit score. These services only work if you actually have errors in your report that you cannot verify or resolve on your own. The main activity of these agencies is to check for inaccuracies in your report which in turn increases your score. This means that their repair services come with both advantages and disadvantages.

Pros

Years of experience, this is the single most important benefit that you can receive from their services. Most individuals may not have enough workable knowledge that can be applied in the repair of their own credit report and score. However, these agencies know the entire system behind the reporting and the scoring. They will know loopholes and techniques that will work on your favor. In fact, they can even identify errors that when made by the credit agency, can be penalized. For example, you are to receive $1000 in damages if a 7 year old negative item is still listed.

Network with creditors, most of these credit repair service agencies already have long term relationships with creditors themselves. This means they can take advantage of any considerations or legitimate exceptions that can be done on your behalf.

Personalized service, since your credit history, performance and report are unique to you, hiring them will offer you a customized service and solution that are fit to your needs. They can take into consideration the other aspects of your financial background, such as income and expense streams, to guide you on making the right decisions for your credit report.

Cons

Cost, this is the main disadvantage of these agencies. Most people who are seeking these services already have problems in their finances. The added expense of the agency's fees may only hurt their finances. However, for some people the benefits that the service provides far outweigh the cost. These agencies also offer money back guarantee in case you are unsatisfied.

Upfront payment, aside from monthly payments, some agencies require an initial payment even before any work is done on your credit report. Some of the amounts are more than $100. It is best that you do your research on any agency before you employ their services.

No guarantees, no legitimate agency can promise that they will be able to increase your scores with their intervention. Since the work usually requires more months of processing, it will cost you more. You may end up with a small increase in your score after months of disputes and investigations.

Chapter 20: Repay Debts And Raise Your Credit Score

Your financial blueprint will be an integral part of your debt repayment strategy. Furthermore, there are a number of actions you should take when planning to repay debts.

·Stick to repayment schedules.

Loans have respective repayment schedules that you must stick to. Otherwise, you end up paying more, due to late fees, penalties, and other charges.

Credit card loans have payment due dates specified the billing statements. Depending on the credit card issuer, there is usually a grace period for paying before the due date where the purchase doesn't incur a finance charge. You do not want to have to pay late fees and exorbitant interest rates due to failure to pay on time.

·Prioritize the debts to be paid.

As much as you want to pay off all your debts all at once, your financial circumstances may not allow it. Therefore, you'll need to prioritize which debts have to be paid first. In order to do that, you must make a list of all your debts, with the relevant information indicated, such as the interest rates, repayment period, balances, and minimum monthly payments, if any.

Here are some options you could look into:

Ø Prioritize debts according to simple interest rates.

In this strategy, you'll pay off the debts with highest interest rates first. You may want to talk to your lender or credit card company to find out if you can have the rate lowered beforehand. This will decrease your monthly minimum, enable you to pay them off faster, and help you save money, as well.

Many credit card companies are willing to lower interests rates to retain customers. It never hurts to ask.

Ø Prioritize debts according to effective interest rates.

Unlike simple interest, effective interest rates take into account the tax effect. This is seen more frequently in student loans, mortgages, and similar loan types.

Prioritize debts according to other fees.

There are some loans or debts that have other fees apart from interest. If the fees are substantial, it could affect your decision on which debt to pay first. There are a few ways to handle these.

·Avoid the "minimum payment syndrome".

Credit card bills give you a minimum payment to keep the account current. Many credit card owners simply pay that amount not realizing the minimum basically only covers the interest. Throwing in an extra $5 can help decrease the principal amount faster.

·Apply the "Snowball" or "Snowflaking" technique.

This is a repayment option applicable to credit card debts (and it's the only instance where paying the minimum monthly payment is actually encouraged). If you have several credit cards, rank them according to their interest rates.

Pay off as much as you can on the first debt – the one with the highest interest rate. Pay the minimum monthly payments on the other credit cards.

Once the first debt has been paid off, move on to the one with the second highest interest rate, paying as much as you can and paying only the minimum monthly payments on the others.

·Negotiate with lenders.

There is nothing wrong with talking to your lenders. Debtors are advised to always be honest with lenders. Relationships that involve lending or borrowing money require a certain level of trust, which is why it is important to be straightforward with them.

Negotiating with lenders can result in better terms. Again, you can ask them to lower your interest rate, which may decrease your minimum payment and make it easier to pay down the principal. You could also ask them lengthen the loan term or period which gives you more time to pay off the debt.

How to Avoid the Negative Impact of Interest

You must be wondering why the debt payment prioritization puts a lot of weight on interest, the amount (which is usually a certain percentage of the amount of principal) to be paid by the debtor to the creditor on top of the principal. It is the fee charged by the lender to a borrower for the use of borrowed money.

Essentially, the concept of interest states that it takes more money to borrow money.

Usually, the interest is calculated into monthly payment, as is the case with car payments and home loans. The interest on credit cards is also factored into the minimum payment.

Interest rates have a negative impact on debt once they begin to increase. As you repay debt, interest rates can pose bigger problems.

For example, the case of credit card debts. As mentioned earlier, a greater chunk of the minimum payments covers the interest more than the original debt. When you are trying to pay off a debt with high interest rates, you will also be paying more toward the finance charge instead of the principal, which means it will take you longer pay off that debt.

The only thing you can do to avoid this is to pay more than the minimum payments specified. Increase your monthly payment so you will be able to pay more of the outstanding principal, which is used as the basis of computing the interest. Naturally, as the amount of outstanding loan decreases, the amount of interest you will pay will also decrease, even if the interest rate remains constant.

Avoid Further Debt

Once you've gotten yourself out of debt, you will probably feel like a weight has been lifted off your shoulders. But it doesn't stop there.

At this stage, you should adopt a "been there, done that, and never again" attitude. You have already experienced what it is like to be saddled with debts, and you have done everything possible in order to be rid of them. Once you've succeeded, it's time to ensure that it never happens again.

Here are very simple tips on how you can continue to have full control over your debt status or, simply, to be free from debt.

1. Use credit cards sparingly.

"Retail therapy" is a very common practice among people who feel down and want to cheer themselves up. The buying process releases dopamine into their systems, which makes them feel happy. It's another reason for shopping addiction.

If shopping is your habit and you are a compulsive spender, use cash instead of credit. If you absolutely must use a credit card, pay off the balance during the grace period, BEFORE interest is attached to the balance, which is usually 28 days after the purchase (check with your credit card company).

Shop only when you truly need to buy something. Do not be easily swayed by ads, brochures and catalogs. If you're the type to buy items and never use them, not only will you save money, you'll also save space in your home.

2. Set some money aside for emergencies.

Experts recommend that everyone have at least six months of living expenses saved up. If you should lose your job today, you'd need to know exactly how you'd keep a roof over your head, food on your table and clothes on yours and your family's backs.

An emergency fund will help keep you from relying on credit cards should you lose your job, your car breaks down or you end up with a huge medical bill.

3. Avoid applying for loans

After paying off a debt, the last thing you want to do is enter into another one. If you must buy something that costs so much that you need to take out a loan, you should consider if it's something you really need. You should consult your financial blueprint, and decide if that loan is worth derailing your financial progress.

4. Look for other sources of additional income.

Bringing in extra money can mitigate debt exponentially. If you have the time or need to supplement your income part-time jobs, garage sales, and small side businesses are a few of the options you could look into. We will discuss potential sources of extra income in a later chapter.

5. Set up a financial documents file.

Receipts, bills, bank statements... anything that has to do with your money, file them accordingly. Keep a log, ledger or file folder of your debts, and update them with payments and other transactions affecting them, complete with the date you made the transaction.

Not only is it prudent recordkeeping; it's also a way to protect yourself should your lenders come after you for a payment you've already made. You will have documentation to back up your dispute (e.g. receipts, bills). You can create your own record keeping system for this.

6. Get help.

There's no shame in seeking help from a professional to learn to manage your credit and your finances.

Approaching a credit counselor for advice can be the best option for a given situation. There are plenty experts who provide credit counseling services to people in serious financial distress. They assess your financial situation and offer reasonable solutions.

Another advantage of using to a credit counselor is their ability to help create a debt management plan. They can find ways to make your debts more manageable, so you can be free of them sooner than you thought.

Obtain Credit Reports

Your credit score is the way that most lenders determine whether or not they want to risk loaning you money. It is a measure of your debt-to-income ratio and the way creditors grade your payment history with lenders. Unfortunately too many of us don't know our credit scores and are surprised when we learn that they are not as high as we thought.

In order to raise your credit score, you first have to know who and what you owe. And, the best way to find out and keep an eye on your debt is obtain your credit reports from each of the three credit reporting bureaus. Once a year, consumers are allowed a free report from each of these companies: TransUnion, Equifax and Experian.

Creditors report to at least one of these companies. The bureaus keep track of how much you each creditor, if your account is current, and how many days delinquent your account is. This is a great way to find out exactly who you owe if you can't remember all the loans and accounts you have opened.

By monitoring your reports you can also catch any inaccuracies that might bring down your credit score. If you find any false or outdated information, you can dispute it to have it removed from your report. 25% of people find incorrect information on their reports.

Another method to monitor your score is to sign up with a credit monitoring service. Credit Karma is a free service that provides your TransUnion and Equifax scores as well as notifies you when a change has been made to your credit report.

Repaying debts is the first way to improve your credit score. The next way is to establish a good payment history. When you begin paying off your debts, you establish a payment history that each creditor reports to the bureaus. The better your repayment history, the more your score improves. Since you can only receive each report once a year, you might want to stagger your requests. This way you'll be able to monitor one report every four months.

Example:

In January you request your report from Experian. Then, you request your report from Equifax in May. Finally you request your report from Transunion in September. This keeps your reports revolving so you can monitor any new activity and dispute any new negative information.

Chapter 21: Rebuilding Your Score After A

Credit Disaster

Getting on the road to improvement with your credit seems like a battle, but the fact is it took many years to screw up your credit and it is going to take years to get back to a good standing. Here are some methods to help you on your way. If you are looking to start rebuilding your credit, one of the first things you should do is get a copy of your credit report. You want to review it not only to see where you are but also check for any potential errors. If there are errors more than likely they are hurting your score and if removed could give you an initial boost.

Moving on, the most important commitment you must make is to never pay your bills late. Your payment history makes up the largest portion of your credit score and paying late will kill your chances for improvement. A monthly budget is a great tool to make sure you have the money to pay your bills and you do it on time. Also, if you not current with any of your accounts you must do anything you can to get current.

The next step is to develop a plan to reduce the amount of debt you have. Your debt to credit ratio is the next largest portion of your credit score and carry high debt will hold you back. From here on out, you must not spend on your credit cards and use your budget to find money to apply to your debt. If you want a jump start, you should have a sale on eBay to sell everything that is not bolted down or even get a second job.

So what happens if you had to file for bankruptcy or have a lot of negative marks on your credit report? Some people get discouraged after being turned down for credit or loans and just give up. Other people who know how the credit system works can start building their credit back up. How fast you can recover from your mistakes depends on you and what you do right away. Understanding how the system works gives you the advantage of time. When you're given a fresh start, you can put the past behind you right away. Credit scoring formulas are more concerned with what you've done recently than what has happened in the past, so it's important to get started off right. Rebuilding your score will still take some time, but if done right, you could significantly boost your score within a couple years. If it's been about seven years since your last negative mark (or up to ten years for a Chapter 7 bankruptcy), your credit score could be above average.

Part 1: Credit Report Repair

People who have had credit problems are sometimes afraid to look at their credit report knowing they won't like what they will see. You might find out that not every little problem was reported in the first place, or you could find that everything was. It is important that you look at your report so that you know what you have to do to help clean it up. For example, you could be the victim of a shady collection agency that has illegally "re-aged" a bad debt. This is when they take an older bad debt and try to make it look more recent than it really is to the credit bureaus. You should know that there are steps to help you clean up your report, and fight back against illegal tactics.

Check Your Report For Serious Errors - As mentioned, you should first get copies of your credit report from the three different agencies. It is important to note that you should get three separate reports, not the 3-in-1 or tri-merged reports, which don't contain all of the information you would get from the three separate reports. Things that you should look for are:

Delinquencies that are older than seven years or accounts listed as delinquent that don't include the date of delinquency Bankruptcies that are older than 10 years or that aren't listed in the specific chapter Judgements or paid liens older than seven years, paid-off debts listed as unpaid

Accounts that were wiped up by a bankruptcy filing still listed as "past due" instead of as "included in bankruptcy"

More than one collection account for the same debt

Collection accounts that don't show the date that the original account went delinquent

Any accounts, delinquencies, collections, etc., that aren't yours

When you do decide to dispute any errors with the agency, make sure you keep records of it in case you run into any problems.

Know Your Rights

The rights that you have under the Fair Credit Reporting Act are:

1)The right to have your dispute investigated

2) The right to have erroneous information corrected

3)The right to a written response

4) The right to have a statement included in your file

5) The right to sue.

Organize Your Attack:

If you have found any errors on your report, you will want to gather any evidence you have to dispute them and notify the credit bureaus. You should then follow up with the credit bureaus with a certified letter so that you get a return receipt. This will make sure to get their attention that there is an error and any failure to act would be a violation of the Fair Credit Reporting Act and grounds for a lawsuit. Usually, the credit bureaus will make the corrections. However, you should still monitor your credit reports to make sure the same error(s) doesn't come up again in the future. This is why it is important to keep records of everything and could help you get it removed more quickly in the future. If the credit bureau is still stating that there is no error, you could always try hiring a lawyer. Sometimes a letter from them will be enough to get it fixed, otherwise, there is always the option of a lawsuit. If you need a referral for an attorney.

Unpaid Debts And Collections:

When it comes to collections, another part of the Fair Debt Collection Practices Act is that you have the right to have a collection account "validated." This means that the collector must prove that the debt is your responsibility and that they have the right to collect it from you. They also have to stop all collection activity until the provide evidence to you. If they are unable to do this, they must cease active collections and stop reporting the debt to the credit bureaus. It is important to note that this only applies to the collection agencies, not the original creditor. To validate a debt, the collector needs to get documentation from the original creditor to prove that you do owe the money. A lot of times, collectors don't have the documentation needed, as some debts have been transferred from different agencies. This process could help get rid of any accounts

that truly don't belong to you or also get
rid of some that actually do.

Conclusion

Having bad credit is usually either the result of bad decisions made over a long period of time or lacking enough emergency funds to take care of a sudden financial challenge. It's important to remove the causes of your credit woes as soon as possible before starting out on your credit repair efforts. This will likely mean that you need to increase your income and decrease your debts and your spending. Consider that if you have sufficient income and your debts and spending are low, you will no longer have the kinds of financial pressures and stresses that you once had. Once you have dealt with the cause of your financial disaster, establish your emergency fund, even if it is only $50 to start with. Stopping spending all of your money each paycheck and starting to save will be the biggest turning point in your financial situation. Once you can start paying down debt and saving, you and your family will be well on your way to starting to achieve your financial goals. While you are working to pay down your debt, the other avenue of your approach to creating a better financial future will be to focus on removing the negative items from your credit report. The laws in reference to this issue favor you, the consumer, even though the prospect of dealing with your credit card companies can be very intimidating. Companies take full advantage of the laws all the time, but for once, things are in your favor. Use these credit laws in a way that supports you and your family. Be aggressive; now is one of those times that being aggressive is appropriate. Get new credit, even if it means establishing secured accounts, and maintain a stellar payment record. Your credit report will show that your financially troubled times are behind you. You can rebuild your credit after financial disaster! The sooner you start, the sooner you'll reap the benefits.

www.ingramcontent.com/pod-product-compliance
Lightning Source LLC
Chambersburg PA
CBHW071213210326
41597CB00016B/1790